LITURGY AND TRADITION

LITURGY AND TRADITION

Theological Reflections of
Alexander Schmemann

edited by
Thomas Fisch

ST VLADIMIR'S SEMINARY PRESS
Crestwood, New York, 10707-1699
1990

This publication is made possible through the generosity of
PAUL STEPHEN BORKOWSKI
a member of SS Peter and Paul Orthodox Church,
South River, New Jersey.
In gratitude to St Vladimir's Orthodox Theological Seminary, as
a center of Orthodox studies in America,
and in memory of that great Teacher,
Father Alexander Schmemann.
May his memory be eternal.

Library of Congress Cataloging-in-Publication Data

Schmemann, Alexander, 1921–1983.
  Liturgy and tradition : theological reflections of Alexander Schmemann /
edited by Thomas Fisch.
    p.   cm.
  Includes responses by B. Botte and W. Jardine Grisbrooke.
  Includes bibliographical references and index.
  ISBN 0-88141-082-9
  1. Orthodox Eastern Church—Liturgy. 2. Orthodox Eastern Church—
Doctrines. 3. Liturgics.   I. Fisch, Thomas, 1946– . II. Title.
BX350.S365 1990
264'.001—dc20   90–36280 CIP

LITURGY AND TRADITION

ISBN 0-88141-082-9

Typeset at St Vladimir's Seminary on a Northgate 386/20 and a QMS PS810
using Ventura Publisher Professional 2.0 in Adobe Garamond 12pt on 13.5pt.

PRINTED IN THE UNITED STATES OF AMERICA

Table of Contents

Introduction

Schmemann's Theological Contribution to the Liturgical Renewal of the Churches

Thomas Fisch
The Saint Paul Seminary School of Divinity
College of St Thomas, St Paul, Minneso ;

The value of Alexander Schmemann's contribution to the liturgical renewal of the churches of East and West can be assessed only within the context of the history of the liturgical movement. It was fortunate for all churches that during the first part of this century an encounter took place in France between members of the Catholic liturgical movement and the Russian Orthodox exile community. Since at least the time of Beauduin, the western liturgical movement has tended to turn toward the East. Similarly, Orthodoxy in Russia has a long history of contact with the West. In Paris in the 1940s, Orthodox emigrés to the West encountered Catholic reformers looking Eastward, and so began a stimulating and fruitful dialogue which continues today. The present essay traces Schmemann's relationship to the liturgical movement, its formative influence on him, and the contributions he in turn has made to it, in particular his definition and understanding of liturgical theology.

His final essay on liturgical theology,[1] bequeathed to us in 1981, calls the churches to reassimilate the foundational goals of

---

1. Chapter 10 (pp. 137–144) of the present volume.

the popular liturgical movement launched by Lambert Beauduin in 1909.[2] Since its origin, the overarching objective of the liturgical movement has been the theological renewal of the church. Consistently it has perceived its work for liturgical revival as an intrinsically theological enterprise. While dedicated to the revitalized participation of the baptized in the liturgy and to their reappropriation of the liturgy's symbolic meanings, the liturgical movement remains oriented to this more profound purpose as well. Beauduin described this part of the movement's agenda in his fundamental book, *La Piété de l'Église*, in 1914.

> The piety of the Christian people, and hence their actions and life, are not grounded sufficiently in the fundamental truths that constitute the soul of the liturgy; that is, the destiny of all things unto the glory of the Father, the Son and the Holy Ghost; the necessary and universal contemplation of Jesus Christ; the central place of the Eucharistic Sacrifice in the Christian life; the mission of the hierarchy in regard to our union with God; the visible realization of the Communion of the Saints. All these truths, which find expression in every liturgical act, are asleep in men's souls; the faithful have lost consciousness of them. Let us change the routine and monotonous assistance at acts of worship into an active and intelligent participation; let us teach the faithful to pray and confess these truths in a body: and the liturgy thus practiced will insensibly arouse a slumbering faith and give a new efficacy, both in prayer and action, to the latent energies of the baptised souls: "the true Christian spirit will flourish again and maintain itself among the faithful."[3]

The ultimate goal of the liturgical movement is an ever more thorough and deep-reaching return to the catholic Tradition, a

---

2. Beauduin called for the creation of a popular liturgical movement in a speech given at the National Congress of Catholic Works held at Malines, Belgium, in September, 1909. Sonya A Quitslund, *Beauduin, A Prophet Vindicated*, New York: Newman Press, 1973, pp. 20-25.

3. Lambert Beauduin, O.S.B., *Liturgy the Life of the Church*, Popular Liturgical Library series I, number 1, Collegeville, MN, The Liturgical Press, 1926, pp. 10-11. This inaugural publication of the Liturgical Press is Virgil Michel's translation of Beauduin's major work, *La Piété de l'Église*, Louvain, Mont César, 1914.

recovery of the liturgy as the center of the church's life.[4]

This concern for the inner meaning of the liturgy was not confined to the European branch of the movement but, from its inception, characterized its North American counterpart as well. When William Busch in 1925 called for the establishment of the liturgical movement in North America he described its goals in similar terms.

> ... I do not take the liturgical movement to mean a mere effort toward improvement of religious externals ... I have chiefly in mind its inner meaning, as a spiritual force as the prayer-life of the Church, the mystical body of Christ, as ultimately the stirring of the Holy Spirit in that body of which Christ is the head and we the members.[5]

For its early leaders the all-important thing was the movement's inner objective, the reappropriation by all the faithful of the heart of the church's life, her liturgical worship. As Busch points out, it is there that "we will find the norm of our prayer life, the *lex orandi.*"[6]

Today the western churches experience the results of the liturgical movement, including the Catholic reforms of Vatican II and the many Protestant liturgical revisions. Within Orthodoxy too there has developed a renewed sense of the centrality of the liturgy in all aspects of the church's life and thought. Throughout the churches there is a gradual and increasingly widespread move towards more frequent communion and more vigorous participation by the whole congregation. All these developments fulfill the vision of the liturgical movement's founders.

4. *Ibid.,* pp. 42 and 44.
5. William Busch, "The Liturgical Movement," Proceedings of the Catholic Educational Association, Twenty-Second Annual Meeting, Pittsburgh, PA, June 29-July 2, 1925, *The Catholic Educational Association Bulletin,* 22, Nov. 1925, p. 670. Busch came into contact with the European movement in the years 1911-1913 while in graduate studies at Louvain. Busch, "Past Present and Future," *Orate Fratres,* 25, 1925, pp. 481-2. He returned to the Saint Paul Seminary (St Paul, MN) where he taught Church History and Liturgy and worked for the liturgical renewal until his death there in 1971.
6. *Ibid.,* pp. 678 and 685.

But the liturgical renewal, for all its beneficial effects in the church's life, has led as well to a liturgical crisis, a crisis which itself is theological in nature. Schmemann rightly observes that, in spite of their having embraced external liturgical revision and renewal, many of the churches have yet to fully welcome the theological component of the liturgical movement's fundamental vision. For the most part, the deeper level of liturgical reform remains elusive.

Reflection on the theological aspect of the liturgy was the focus of Alexander Schmemann's intellectual life. He intuitively grasped and insisted upon the essentially theological character of all liturgical renewal. He recognized that the renewal of the churches requires a rediscovery of the liturgy's own inherent theology, that same theology which once informed the whole of the church's life as well as the teachings and writings of the leaders of the Patristic age. This theological content which is inherent in the liturgy itself is named by Schmemann "liturgical theology." In order to appreciate his significance as a liturgical theologian, it is important to review briefly his scholarly origins.

Schmemann received his intellectual formation in Paris during the 1940s. Sergius Bulgakov, Anton Kartashev, and Cyprian Kern were among his teachers. He was also strongly influenced by Nicholas Afanassiev. But, as Fr John Meyendorff points out in the final essay of the present volume, Schmemann was in contact as well with a wider theological community in Paris. At the very moment when the liturgical and patristic revival began to flourish within the western church, Schmemann was in touch with the heart of that revival. Within this circle, Jean Daniélou and Louis Bouyer were particularly influential on the developing young theologian. In the words of Fr Meyendorff, "It is from that existing milieu that Fr Schmemann really learned 'liturgical theology,' a 'philosophy of time' and the true meaning of the 'paschal mystery'." [7]

7. John Meyendorff, "A Life Worth Living," p. 149 below.

It was in Paris, particularly under the influence of Louis Bouyer, that Schmemann began to reflect at length upon what he later defined as liturgical theology. From the beginning, the liturgical movement had been attentive to the theological dimension of the liturgy. Various thinkers including Bouyer, I-H Dalmais and Cyprian Vaggagini made important contributions to rediscovering this dimension.[8] But where those writers employed the expressions "liturgical theology" and "theology of the liturgy" interchangeably, Schmemann, already in 1957, began to formulate a distinction between them which has become the basis for today's accepted terminology within the field of liturgical studies.[9] This distinction is the touchstone of his contribution to the churches. Liturgical theology has a long history in the life of the church, but Schmemann is the first to articulate its nature precisely and to distinguish it from other forms of theology which employ the liturgy as a "source."

The term "liturgical theology" appears as early as 1937 in M Cappuyns' paper "Liturgie et théologie" presented that year at the Liturgical Week at Mt César, Belgium.[10] Here and elsewhere, however, the terms "liturgical theology" and "theology of the liturgy" are used as synonyms. For example, in *Liturgical Piety* (1955), when treating "the theological study of the liturgy,"

8. For example, Louis Bouyer, *Liturgical Piety*, Notre Dame, IN, University of Notre Dame Press, 1955; I-H Dalmais, "Liturgy and the Mystery of Salvation" in *The Church at Prayer*, Vol I: *Introduction to the Liturgy*, English translation of *l'Église en prière*, 3rd edition, Paris, Desclée, 1968; and Cyprian Vaggagini, *Theological Dimensions of the Liturgy*, Collegeville, MN, The Liturgical Press, 1976.

9. The distinction is set forth in detail in his essay "Liturgical Theology: Its Task and Method," SVSQ 1:4, 1957, pp. 16-27, reprinted as chapter 1 of his book *Introduction to Liturgical Theology*, London, Faith Press, 1966, originally published in Russian, Paris, 1961.

10. M. Cappuyns, "Liturgie et théologie," in *La vrai visage de la liturgie*, Cours et conférences des semaines liturgiques, Louvain, Abbaye de Mont César, 1938, pp. 175-209. See in particular p. 199.

Bouyer speaks in the following way:

> The theology of liturgy is the science which begins with the liturgy itself in order to give a theological explanation of what the liturgy is, and of what is implied in its rites and words. Those authors are not to be accounted liturgical theologians, therefore, who go on to work the other way round and seek to impose on liturgy a ready-made explanation which pays little or no attention to what the liturgy says about itself.[11]

Here is the fundamental insight. Schmemann seized upon this distinction of Bouyer, refined it and gradually enunciated it more clearly during the years 1957–69.

In 1957 he published "Liturgical Theology: Its Task and Method,"[12] in which he describes liturgical theology as "the elucidation of the theological meaning of worship." He views liturgical theology as analogous to Biblical theology, a field in its own right.[13]

> Liturgical theology is therefore an independent theological discipline with its own special subject — the liturgical tradition of the church, and requiring its corresponding and special method, distinct from the methods of other theological disciplines.[14]

This understanding is refined in the 1963 essay "Theology and Liturgical Tradition," where he clearly distinguishes "liturgical theology" from "theology of the liturgy." The former is an enterprise in which the liturgy "must be the basic *source* of theological thinking." In the latter the liturgy necessarily remains an *object* of theology, even to the extent that it is "an object requiring, first of all, a theological clarification of its nature and function."[15]

Finally in 1969, in response to Bernard Botte and W Jardine Grisbrooke, he comes to the full articulation of this important

---

11. Bouyer, *Liturgical Piety*, Notre Dame, Indiana, University of Notre Dame Press, 1955, p. 277.
12. SVTQ [*St Vladimir's Theological Quarterly*] 1:4, 1957, pp. 16-27; see note 9 above.
13. *Introduction to Liturgical Theology*, second edition, Crestwood, New York, St Vladimir's Seminary Press, 1975, pp. 14-15.
14. *Ibid.*, p. 16.
15. Pp. 11–12 below.

distinction. In "Liturgical Theology, Theology of Liturgy, and Liturgical Reform," he contrasts "theology of liturgy," that part of theology which has the liturgy as its specific *object*, with "liturgical theology" understood as "first of all and above everything else, the attempt to grasp the theology revealed *in* and through the liturgy itself."[16] Schmemann contends that there is "a radical and irreducible difference between these two." His formulation of this important distinction is the hallmark of his thought as well as the principal contribution he makes to the liturgical renewal.

His second major contribution consists in his liturgical theology itself. There is not space here to summarize that body of work. It must suffice to point out two major features of his theology which are of particular importance to the liturgical renewal. The first of these is his rediscovery of the *eschatology* inherent to the liturgy. The second is his articulation of the early church's consciousness of the relationship between the *ecclesia*, the eucharist, and the eighth day, a consciousness which continues to be embodied in the liturgical tradition of both East and West.

Schmemann considers the recovery of the eschatological dimension of the liturgy to be one of the main tasks of the liturgical movement.[17] His statement of this goal reveals his assumption that the liturgy is an eschatological reality. He perceives the church's experience of itself as an experience primarily given and received in the liturgy. This movement of self-realization on the part of the church is essentially an eschatological experience since it is within the liturgical event that the church experiences herself as the manifestation of the Reign of God in the world.[18] The essential function of the liturgy is to bring the church into being, "to *realize* the church by revealing her (to herself and to the world) as the epiphany of the Kingdom of God."[19]

16. P. 39 below
17. "The Liturgical Revival and the Orthodox Church," p. 114 below.
18. "Liturgy and Theology," pp. 54–56 below.
19. "Liturgical Theology, Remarks on Method," p. 142 below.

This Kingdom, which for "this world" is *yet to come* and forms the ultimate horizon of its history, is already present (revealed, communicated, given, accepted, ...) in the Church. And it is the liturgy which accomplishes this presence and this parousia, and which, in this sense (in its totality) is the *sacrament of the church* and thus the *sacrament of the Kingdom*.[20]

The eschatological character of Christian faith has not been lost, as some may think. The liturgy continues to embody the eschatological consciousness of the early church. It is Schmemann's insight that eschatology, far from being a small or accidental aspect of the liturgy, is in fact what defines the liturgy. The "specificity" of the Christian liturgy "consists in its eschatological character."[21]

This realization that the liturgy is the "breaking into the present" of the world to come begins to explain the second notable feature of Schmemann's liturgical theology, his articulation of the relationship between the *ecclesia*, the eucharist, and the eighth day. Amid the many studies produced in recent years on the church, on the eucharist, and on the early church's eschatological consciousness, Schmemann alone perceives and enunciates the interconnection of these three things within the living church's experience and its celebration of the liturgy. His insight is that the early church's vision and experience of itself, the world and the Kingdom of God was a unitary experience. In the mind of the early church these three were so integrally interrelated as to be perceived as three aspects of a single experiential reality.

In was within the early church's celebration of the liturgy that the connection and interdependence of these three realities was experienced as self-evident. How do we know this and what is the record of that experience? The evidence lies in the early church's sense of the eighth day, the Day of the Lord, which the church perceived as revealed in and through an encounter with the Risen

20. *Ibid.*, pp. 142–143.
21. *Ibid.*, p. 142.

Christ within the eucharistic assembly (*ecclesia*) on the first and eighth day of the week. The assembly came together to meet the glorified Lord (the personal embodiment of the Reign of God) within the eucharistic event. Eucharist, eschatological Day, Assembly; for the early church these were one reality.[22] Again, this remains true at the heart of the liturgy to the present day. Schmemann is convinced that "this connection still exists *liturgically*, but ... it is neither understood nor experienced in the way it was understood and experienced in the early church."[23]

The recognition of the fundamental unity of these three realities and the history of their gradual divergence into three nearly totally separate entities in the consciousness of the later church is an insight of immense heuristic value. At once it illuminates the present state of the Christian tradition, it aids in recovering the perspective of the early church, it unlocks a deeper level of meaning within the liturgy, and it serves to demythologize many seemingly untouchable institutional structures. The fact that one insight bears such a range and depth of effects is enough to demonstrate its value.

This quick sketch of Alexander Schmemann's contribution to the liturgical renewal of the church begins to reveal the silhouette of his theological stature. He is responsible for the precise definition of liturgical theology as well as for the pioneering reflection on the task and method of the field which bears that name. In addition he offers his own perceptive and profound liturgical theology of which only two important features have been mentioned here.

For the contemporary churches to be faithful to the vision of the liturgical movement's founders, the original theological goals of that movement must again receive attention. Any reconsidera-

22. "Liturgical Theology, Theology of Liturgy, and Liturgical Reform," pp. 41–42 below.
23. *Ibid.*

tion of this theological agenda must acknowledge Schmemann's liturgical theology. He presents key insights which can serve as a bracing stimulus for the continuing liturgical renewal and a means of fulfilling the theological goal of the liturgical movement.

Schmemann has produced an important synthesis which deserves consideration by all students of the liturgy. This collection of some of his major essays is intended as a companion volume to *Introduction to Liturgical Theology.*[24] It exhibits the full range of his thinking on liturgical theology and serves as a memorial tribute to a most important theologian of the twentieth century church.

24. For his complete bibliography see Paul Garrett, "Fr Alexander Schmemann: A Chronological Bibliography," SVTQ, 28, 1984, p. 11-26.

1

Theology and Liturgical Tradition

The problem of the relationship between worship and theology is on the theological agenda of our time.[1] Several factors, moreover, seem to indicate that it is an urgent problem — the victorious growth of liturgical movements in practically all Christian denominations, the ecumenical encounter,[2] the rediscovery of symbolism as an essential religious category, and, finally, the theological revival with its radical *examen de conscience* concerning the very nature of theological inquiry. The *leitourgia* of the Church has become for the theologian a challenge that has to be evaluated and answered in theological terms. And even those who denounce this growing interest in worship as dangerous (e.g. Karl Barth) must do so on theological grounds, within a consistent theology of worship.

Although the existence of the problem is certain, it is still difficult to define it. There is much confusion and ambiguity in the use of certain terms. One speaks, for example, of liturgical theology, of a liturgical "resourcement" of theology. For some, this implies an almost radical rethinking of the very concept of theology, a complete change in its structure. The *leitourgia* — being the unique expression of the Church, of its faith and of its life — must become the basic source of theological thinking, a

1. From *Worship in Scripture and Tradition*, edited by Massey Hamilton Shepherd, Jr. Copyright © 1963 by Oxford University Press, Inc. Reprinted by permission.
2. According to Professor Joseph Sittler, it acknowledges "the fact that the way Christian people worship is declarative of what they believe. This declaration as made in worship may well be of a depth and fullness seldom attained in credal propositions."

kind of *locus theologicus par excellence*. There are those, on the other hand, who, while admitting the importance of the liturgical experience for theology, would rather consider it as a necessary *object* of theology — an object requiring, first of all, a theological clarification of its nature and function. Liturgical theology or the theology of liturgy — we have here two entirely different views concerning the relationship between worship and theology. And this difference implies much more than a difference of emphasis. Our attempt here is designed to clarify, very briefly and, so to say, tentatively, at least a few of these implications.

I

To understand the real nature of the two tendencies mentioned here, we must remember that both have antecedents in the past, and are based to some extent on a conscientious desire to recover positions that are supposed to have been held previously. And, indeed, one can discern in the history of the Church two main types or patterns of relationship between theology and the *leitourgia*.

(1) *The patristic type.* The recent revival of patristic studies shows that one of the major characteristics of the Fathers is precisely that of an organic connection between their theological thought and their liturgical experience. *Lex orandi est lex credendi:* this axiom means that the liturgical tradition, the liturgical life, is a natural milieu for theology, its self-evident term of reference. The Fathers do not "reflect" on liturgy. For them it is not an *object* of theological inquiry and definition, but rather the living source and the ultimate criterion of all Christian thought: "Our opinion is in accordance with the Eucharist, and the Eucharist in turn establishes our opinion," said St Irenaeus.[3] We shall have to deal with this position later on. At this point let us simply state that it

---

3. *Adv. haer.* iv. 18, 5: *Nostra autem consonans est sententia Eucharistiae, et Eucharistia rursus confirmat sententiam nostram.*

existed, and that there is nothing fortuitous in the claim sometimes put forward by the liturgical movement that it constitutes a return to this patristic ideal.

(2) *The scholastic type.* By "scholastic" we mean, in this instance, not a definite school or period in the history of theology, but a theological structure which existed in various forms in both the West and the East, and in which all "organic" connection with worship is severed. Theology here has an independent, rational status; it is a search for a system of consistent categories and concepts: *intellectus fidei.* The position of worship in relation to theology is reversed: from a *source* it becomes an *object,* which has to be defined and evaluated within the accepted categories (e.g. definitions of sacraments). Liturgy supplies theology with "data," but the method of dealing with these data is independent of any liturgical context. Moreover, the selection and classification of the data themselves are already a "product" of the accepted conceptual structure.

From the point of view which interests us here, it is of paramount importance that, in spite of all the developments and variations of Christian theology, it is this second type that has had a monopoly from the end of the patristic age up to our own time. A good example is the Eastern Orthodox Church, justly considered to be the liturgical Church *par excellence.* The student of Orthodox theology knows that in all its post-patristic developments — late Byzantine theology (with the possible exception of the "hesychast" movement), the school of Kiev in the sixteenth-seventeenth centuries, Russian "academic" theology, contemporary Greece, etc. — liturgical tradition has played practically no role, and has been almost totally ignored, even as a *locus theologicus.* Liturgy and theology have peacefully co-existed — the former in its traditional form, the latter as a sacred science — with no attempt made to correlate their respective languages.

In the West the situation was somewhat different. Instead of a peaceful co-existence, there was a direct impact of theological speculation (medieval, post-tridentine) on the very forms of liturgical life. The changes were so substantial that, according to some Roman Catholic leaders of the liturgical movement, nothing short of a real liturgical reformation can restore the true liturgical tradition. The Reformers protested against the medieval theology of worship, but in spite of their desire for a return to the primitive tradition, they actually replaced this medieval doctrine by another theology of worship, so that in the Protestant Churches the *leitourgia* remained a function of its theological conception and interpretation. Subsequent developments in Roman Catholic and Protestant theology did not alter this situation. Intellectual or anti-intellectual, liberal or pietistic, theology not only remained internally independent of worship, but claimed the right to control it, and to form it according to the *lex credendi*.

The liturgical movement is the first attempt to break this monopoly, to restore to liturgical tradition its own theological status. In this it radically differs from all ritualistic or pietistic revivals of the past, with their emphasis on the psychology or the edifyingly mystical atmosphere of worship — on the "mood setting devices made available by the application of psychological categories," to quote Professor Sittler. Its fundamental presupposition is that the liturgy not only has a theological meaning and is declarative of faith, but that it is the living norm of theology; it is in the liturgy that the sources of faith — the Bible and tradition — become a living reality. The leaders and participants of the liturgical movement advocate a return to what they consider to be the essence of the patristic age, and in the name of this return denounce the other, the scholastic type, as a deviation from the genuine Christian norm of theology.

II

It is at this point that the question must be asked: Can either of these two attitudes, in their pure expression, be acceptable to us today, and be the starting point of a reconsideration of the relationship between worship and theology? It seems to me that in the modern discussion of the liturgical problem, one essential fact is very often overlooked, or at least not given sufficient attention. Yet it is this fact that makes the liturgical problem of our time much more complex than it may seem. I define it as the *metamorphosis of the liturgical consciousness.*

When we speak of "liturgical tradition" of the early Church (the one implied in patristic theology) we must keep in mind that this tradition was constituted by two basic elements, equally essential for its proper understanding: (a) a formal continuity of Christian *leitourgia* with the Jewish worship, which supplied the Church with the basic liturgical structures (the *"ordo"* or *"typos,"* the liturgical language); and (b) the radical transformation of the spirt of worship — i.e. of the meaning attached to these structures and forms. Both elements have been studied and stressed in many recent works on the history of Christian worship, but it seems to me that not all the necessary conclusions have been drawn. Yet it is only when these two fundamental categories are seen in their relationship to each other that one can understand the real nature of the patristic use of liturgy, and also of the *metamorphosis* which marked the post-patristic liturgical development.

We know today that the cult of the early Church was essentially a Jewish cult, that practically all its forms can be traced back to Jewish antecedents, including the sacramental worship which was for a long time ascribed to the non-Jewish "mystery cults" of the Graeco-Roman world. Every year some new study widens and strengthens our knowledge of the Jewish background and the Jewish connotations of early Christian liturgy. But the liturgiologists and the historians to whom we are indebted for these studies are not always aware that this formal continuity implied a radical transformation in terms of a new content put in the old forms, of a Christian cult growing from Judaic roots. The Jewish *Kiddusha*[4] gives its pattern to the Christian Eucharist, the Jewish baptism — whatever it was — to the Christian baptism. But the transformation remains within "cultic" categories; it is a transformation of the cult. In fact, this transformation took place at a much deeper level, and this seems to me the essential fact in the formation of the Christian liturgical tradition.

Paradoxically, to make a long story short, one can say that this transformation consists in the *abolishment of cult as such*, or at least in the complete destruction of the old philosophy of cult. The Christian *leitourgia* is not a "cult" if by this term we mean a sacred action, or rite, performed in order to establish "contact" between the community and God, whatever the meaning and the nature of such contact. A "cult" by its very essence presupposes a radical distinction between the "sacred" and the "profane," and, being a means of reaching or expressing the "sacred," it posits all the non-sacred as "profane." The Jewish worship was a cult in the deepest meaning of this term. In spite of all its uniqueness, of all its opposition to pagan cults, it shared with the latter this basic distinction between the "sacred" and the "profane," this function of being a means of communication between the "sacred" and the "profane." It was based on a priestly order, and on the principle of a complete isolation of the cultic action from the "profane" areas of life.

From this point of view the Christian *leitourgia* did not originate as a cult. It was not a cult, because within the *ecclesia* — the royal priesthood, the holy people, the peculiar nation — the distinction between the sacred and the profane, which is the very condition of cult, has been abolished. The Church is not a natural community which is "sanctified" through the cult. In its essence the Church is the presence, the actualization in this world of the

---

4. The blessings or *berakoth* recited over "the cup of blessing" during the Jewish ceremonial meal.

"world to come," in this *aeon* — of the Kingdom. And the mode of this presence, of this actualization of the new life, the new *aeon*, is precisely the *leitourgia.* It is only within this eschatological dimension of the Church that one can understand the nature of the liturgy: to actualize and realize the identity of the *ecclesia* with the new *aeon*, of the "age to come."

> Thou didst not cease to do all things until thou hadst brought us back to heaven and hadst endowed us with thy kingdom which is to come. (Anaphora of St John Chrysostom)

The *leitourgia*, therefore, is not a cultic action performed in the Church, on its behalf, and for it; it is the action of the Church itself, or the Church *in actu*, it is the very expression of its life. It is not opposed to the non-cultic forms or aspects of the *ecclesia*, because the *ecclesia* exists in and through the *leitourgia*, and its whole life is a *leitourgia.* This life is rooted in the sacraments of Baptism and Eucharist, and the sacraments according to the early Christian understanding are precisely the means of the eschatological life of the Church. They manifest the "coming *aeon*" in this world, and they are themselves but the expressions of the Church as the visible sign of the Kingdom which is to come, its anticipation in time and history.

If the *leitourgia* has not only preserved the form of a cult, but can be described as a real continuation of the Jewish cult, it is to be explained in terms of the same Christian eschatology. The latter has been expressed in the antinomical formula: "*in* the world, but not *of* the world." The Church belongs to the age to come, but dwells in "this world," and its proper mission is to witness to the *Eschaton* — the Lordship of Christ until He comes, until the consummation of time. In this world, the *Eschaton* — the holy, the sacred, the "otherness" — can be expressed and manifested only as "cult." Not only in relation to the world, but in relation to itself as dwelling in the world, the Church must use the forms and language of the cult, in order eternally to transcend the cult, to "become what it is." And it is this "transition" of the cult — the cult which itself fulfills the *reality* to which it can only point, which it can announce, but which is the consummation of its function as cult — that we call sacrament.

Thus the liturgical tradition of the Church is fundamentally antinomical in its nature. It is a cult which eternally transcends itself, because it is the cult of a community which eternally realizes itself, as the Body of Christ, as the Church of the Holy Spirit, as ultimately, the new *aeon* of the Kingdom. It is a tradition of forms and structures, but these forms and structures are no longer those of a "cult," but those of the Church itself, of its life "in Christ." Now we can understand the real meaning of the patristic use of liturgical tradition. The formula *lex orandi est lex credendi* means nothing else than that theology is *possible* only within the Church, i.e. as a fruit of this new life in Christ, granted in the sacramental *leitourgia*, as a witness to the eschatological fullness of the Church, as in other terms, a participation in this *leitourgia*. The problem of the relationship between liturgy and theology is not for the Fathers a problem of priority or authority. Liturgical tradition is not an "authority" or a *locus theologicus*; it is the ontological condition of theology, of the proper understanding of *kerygma*, of the Word of God, because it is in the Church, of which the *leitourgia* is the expression and the life, that the sources of theology are functioning as precisely "sources."

III

For reasons that have been partially explained and partially are still to be explained, this understanding of the liturgical tradition has not been preserved within the Church, and it is here that we approach the *metamorphosis* of the liturgical consciousness, mentioned above. It is not Christian worship that changed, but it is comprehension by the believers, by the Christian community. In a simplified form one can say that, in the consciousness of the community, the *leitourgia* became once again a cult, i.e. a system of sacred actions and rites, performed in the Church, for the Church and by the Church, yet in order not to make the Church "what it is," but to "sanctify" individual members of the Church, to bring them into contact with God. The categories of the sacred and the profane came back, and became categories within the Church itself. One can study this transformation from many points of view — the doctrine of ministry, the forms of Church government, the relations between clergy and laity, etc. — but here we shall limit ourselves to the liturgical sphere proper.

The Byzantine period in the history of the Eastern Orthodox worship is a very good example. It was marked by the progressive "sacralization" of the clergy, the appearance of the iconostasis separating the sanctuary from the congregation, and finally the transformation of the *laicos,* the member of the Body of Christ and the citizen of the Kingdom, into the *cosmicos,* or the "layman" in the actual acceptance of this term. The liturgy became a separate activity, a "means of grace" sharply opposed to all other spheres of Church life — which were, in turn, condemned to a progressive "profanization."

This *metamorphosis* deeply marked theological thinking. One example is sufficient. In the study of the Eucharist, theological attention was focused exclusively upon the question: what happens to the elements, and exactly how and when does it happen? For the early Church the real question was: what happens to the *Church* in the Eucharist? The difference is radical; it shows perfectly clearly the nature of the change, from the eschatological to the ecclesiological "dimension" of the sacraments. Theology shifted to a purely "cultic" inquiry, which is centered always on the question of the validity and modality of a rite. Considering the sacrament exclusively from the point of view of the elements (transubstantiation, consubstantiation, etc.), theology practically ignored the liturgy itself, considering it as a non-essential, symbolical "framework" for the minimum of action and words necessary for validity. The whole liturgical action ceased to be understood as *sacramental*, i.e. as a series of transformations ultimately leading the Church, the *ecclesia*, into the fullness of the Kingdom, the only real "condition" of the transformation of the elements.

This *metamorphosis* of the liturgical consciousness makes it impossible to accept the choice between "liturgical theology" and a "theology of the liturgy" as valid. For the liturgy has to be explained once again as the *leitourgia of the Church* — and this is the task of the theologian. But for this task, the real liturgical tradition must be rediscovered — and this is the task of the liturgiologist. If it is for theology to purify the liturgy, it is for the liturgy to give back to theology that eschatological fullness, which the liturgy alone can "actualize" — the participation in the life of the Kingdom which is still to come.

> According to the measure of our possibilities,
> O Christ, our God,
> the Sacrament of thy will,
> has been fulfilled and completed,
> for we have had the memory of thy death,
> we have seen the image of thy resurrection,
> we have been filled with thine eternal life,
> we have enjoyed this immortal food,
> which grant us also in the age to come.
> (Final prayer of the Liturgy of St Basil)

2

The Role of Liturgical Theology:
A Debate
On Liturgical Theology

Bernard Botte, O.S.B.
Abbaye de Mont César, Louvain

The problem of a theology of liturgy has existed in the West as well as in the East since the establishment of seminaries in the Roman Catholic Church.[1] A course in liturgy was given there. One had to teach future priests how to perform with dignity and intelligence the sacred rites of their ministry. It was indeed an essentially practical discipline dealing mainly with rubrics, which were themselves so numerous and precise that no time was left for anything else. And even if someone had desired to add anything, what would it have been? The Roman liturgy became "fixed" in the XIIIth century, i.e. at a time when an abundant parasitic symbolism was flourishing. Good will was needed to accept that the bishop's miter, according to the Roman Pontifical, symbolized the horns of Moses and that the bishops had to appear "awesome" with the two horns of the Old and the New Testament. To be sure all this is marginal to the liturgy; but the very abundance of that kind of detail obscured the essential. When Dom Beauduin, a few years before World War I, had the courage to seek in the liturgy a source of life for the Christian people, he was bitterly criticized by *Études*, the journal of French Jesuits, for it was taken for granted that liturgy is the protocol of public relations with God. In such

---

1. Appeared originally in *St Vladimir's Seminary Quarterly*, 12, 1968, pp. 170-173.

conditions the very question of a theology of liturgy could not emerge.

The situation in the Eastern Church is not exactly the same, and one should avoid one-sided comparisons. Christians of the Byzantine rite were not cut off from the liturgy, as were the Latins, who were kept busy by parallel devotions while the clergy performed rites. One writer has even affirmed that there was not need for a liturgical movement in the Orient because the people there still took an active part in the liturgy. In reality, however, if I understand Father Schmemann,[2] the situation was not radically different. The liturgy was becoming a "thing in itself," and one no longer understood its deep meaning. The Byzantine rite also became "fixed" in the XIIIth century and accidental symbolism grew in it, as it did in the West. The essential was so flooded by the accidental that it was no longer discernible. Then there was also a triumph of ritualism. Yet, a living celebration depends not only on the exactitude of rites, but primarily on the spirit in which they are performed.

The liturgical renewal, in the East as in the West, began with a historical study of worship. It was a necessary stage, which helped to put many things in their real place and to discover the meaning of rites that have become virtually incomprehensible. History revealed, also, the "inadaptation" of certain rites. Thus, for example, in the Latin mass the subdeacon held the paten from the offertory until the commixture because, at an earlier stage, there was placed on the paten the *fermentum* (the bread consecrated by the Pope at a previous mass). The *fermentum*, however, disappeared centuries ago. The rite thus no longer had any meaningful purpose and was but the "witness" of a nonexisting custom. It is the tendency, common to all traditions, to preserve rites which have lost their *raison d'être*. Usually these are secondary details,

---

2. Alexander Schmemann, *Introduction to Liturgical Theology*, London, The Faith Press, Ltd., 1966.

but when their number increases, they finish by obscuring the essential rite, and historical explanations do not make them more understandable.

Historical study is not capable of restoring by its explanations the vital value of the liturgy. It can, however, help the theologian in another way: by distinguishing the essential from the secondary. Rites have developed during some ten centuries and under various influences. What is essential is that which remains from the beginning and persists in spite of subsequent additions. Father Schmemann outlines a history of Byzantine liturgy in three periods. The first one goes from the origins of the liturgy to the Constantinian peace. The second covers the time between Constantine and the IX–Xth centuries and is characterized by the development on the one hand of the "cathedral rite" and on the other hand of monastic liturgy. The third period, after the ninth century, is that of a synthesis, achieved through the liturgical leadership of monks.

Apparently it is the first period that is for Father Schmemann the "golden age." The essential elements are obvious. There is the entire structure of the Eucharistic and sacramental liturgy — which, by its very nature, is extra-temporal — and there is the "sanctification of time," whether of the day, the week, or the year. These two elements do not merely "co-exist" but are united within a synthesis. That these are the essential elements, I have no doubt; and it is here, I am sure, that a theology of liturgy has its starting point. It seems to me, however, that it is dangerous to proclaim one particular age to be the ideal age. One risks then to neglect the legitimate aspects of subsequent development. It seems to me that Father Schmemann has not avoided this danger and that his appreciation of the second period somewhat suffers from it. The contrast between early Christian piety and that of later centuries, between a piety inspired by faith and the one based on the power of worship seems to me somewhat exaggerated. It is wrong to say that "cult" is not a part of the primitive "*kerygma.*" Faith has never been kept a part from Baptism, and did not the Lord himself instruct his disciples at the Last Supper to "do this in remembrance of me?" Is this not the original core of Christian worship? No doubt the growth of a rite always implies the danger of stressing the "accessories" at the expense of the essential. Yet, is this development therefore illegitimate? Are we, for example, to condemn vocal prayer because it is possible to pronounce words without thinking of anything?

The growth of the liturgy was as necessary as that of dogma or institutions. It is a law of life. Yet not all growth is *ipso facto* progress; it can also be a deviation and a distortion. One cannot "canonize" all that has happened and still happens. But beyond individual and passing deviations, can one speak of a fundamental one affecting the entire liturgical tradition? Father Schmemann seems to think so, but he has difficulties in showing where and when it originated. According to him it is not liturgy itself that "deviated" but the spirit of its celebration. There was, he claims, at a certain time a liturgical piety based on a purely "cultic" approach and influenced by mystery cults. While energetically rejecting any affinity of the Christian cult itself with these mysteries, Father Schmemann admits their influence on piety during the post-Constantinian period. But when one speaks of piety, one leaves the objectivity of the cult for the subjectivity of individual reactions. Within the same liturgical assembly one can find both a person with a "magical" idea of cult and another giving it its real meaning. This is a danger threatening all cults. Old Testament prophets protested against ritualistic formalism, and Jesus denounced that of the Pharisees. The mystery cults are for nothing here, and even today we face the same threat. What is implied here is not the liturgy but human weakness. The question is not whether there were Christians who believed in the all powerful nature of cult — for they have always existed and still exist — but whether Christian liturgy was presented as a kind of mystery-cult.

This I do not see. One has to place rites into their context again. Liturgy is the *"locus"* of the Word of God, not only because Scriptures are read, but also because they are explained and commented within liturgy. St John Chrysostom in the East and St Augustine in the West believed in the "efficiency" of rites but also in that of the Word of God. Word and Sacrament were indispensable means in the sanctification of men and the edification of the people of God. We have here neither opposition nor synthesis between two terms of religion but faithfulness to the primitive tradition: "Go, teach all nations, and baptize ..." It is quite possible that at certain times and in certain places the equilibrium was broken and the word of God was neglected. But this does not affect liturgy itself and has nothing to do with the influence of mystery cults.

A third period begins in the IXth century. It is marked by a synthesis between the "cathedral rite" and the monastic liturgy. This distinction comes, it seems to me, from A Baumstark and corresponds to a reality. One must, however, avoid oversimplification here. From the IVth century on monks are seen taking part in the liturgy of Jerusalem. The same phenomenon can be observed in Rome in the VIth century. Monastic piety has obviously influenced liturgical developments. But has this influence been always beneficial, be it in the East or in the West? Liturgical books, for example, have been completed in monastic circles. This is the case of the *Ordines Romani* in the West, of the *Typica* in the East. Here and there it is the time of rubricism and symbolism. Nothing of the past was lost, but much was added. The result was complicated, virtually impracticable, liturgics in which the essential is flooded by the non-essential. This state of affairs will perpetuate itself because after the XIIIth century the liturgical development comes to an end. If there was a liturgical decadence it is at this period that it took place. The essential was preserved but burdened with much dead weight. This is true of the East as of the West. Think, for instance, of the minor orders of doorkeepers or exorcists which respond to no real function but which continue to be conferred.

If I have demonstrated some reservations about Fr Schmemann's treatment of the liturgical development, I fully agree with him on the role of liturgical theology. Its task is to recover the essential elements. History is not enough, for it supplies data but is not competent to issue value judgements. It is not enough to look to the past in order to find there an ideal age and suppress all that followed. There are developments which are legitimate and useful for the life of the Church, and even a "modern" addition can be publicly justified. The essential here is that it be in continuity with the initial impulse. We have here an analogy with dogmatic development. The liturgical development was not less important, and to judge it there is only one criterion: Tradition. In spite of divergences among various churches, a vast area of agreement does exist. It is within this consensus that one is to look for the essential. It also supplies the criterion for the evaluation of all subsequent developments.

The task of liturgical theology is then to recover the essential and to relegate the "accessories" to their place. Does that imply a liturgical reform? This is what happened to Roman liturgy. A return to fundamental principles has resulted in a "cleaning-up" as well as in new creativity. One has discovered that rigid forms were no longer adequate either to the essence of liturgy or the needs of the Christian people. Is a similar development possible and desirable within Byzantine liturgy? I am not competent to answer this question. The situation here is different from that of the Roman liturgy, where "rubrics" had an absolute rigidity. The Eastern Church has always preserved a certain flexibility, but the freedom of a Byzantine celebrant is not limitless. Does the East need a reform? Is this the time for it? One understands perfectly well the hesitations and oppositions. The Roman reform was in preparation for half a century, but one can still ask whether things did not go too fast. The change was too abrupt and the mania for experimentation has resulted here and there in anarchy. One understands quite well that this example is a source for hesitation for the Easterners. Premature or one-sided reforms might do more harm than good. And yet is the idea of a reform to be rejected altogether? Ought not liturgical theology to prepare the funda-mental principles of a reform in continuity with, and respectful of, Tradition? To this question Father Schmemann is more quali-fied to give an answer.

✺ ✺ ✺

A Brief Response

Alexander Schmemann

Dom Botte seems to me to have misunderstood somewhat the concept, central in my book, of liturgical piety.[3] For him it is the "subjective" reaction to cult, as distinct from the latter's "objective" character, which alone is the object of liturgical study and evaluation. My main point is that liturgical piety is also an "objective" datum, although obviously different from the more formal data of cultic forms themselves. If, for example, during nearly a thousand years the idea of communion as not only an individual but also a corporate act has virtually disappeared from the mind of both clergy and laity, and this in spite of the liturgical "*ordo*" or structure which remain "corporate" minded ("... and unite all of us who partake of the same Bread and Chalice one to another ..."), is it an "individual" and "subjective" phenomenon or a very real and indeed *objective* shift in liturgical piety? Can one

---

3. This reply to Bernard Botte appeared in the same issue of the *St Vladimir's Seminary Quarterly*, 12, 1968, pp. 173–4.

disregard it and simply point to the "norm" without, at first, evaluating it and trying to find its deep causes? To deny that the category of the "awesome," "terrible," etc., which is unknown to the early tradition yet is so obvious in the later one, has something to do not with the "mystery-cults" as such, but with religious mentality which made these cults popular, is to my mind, wrong. That a further study is needed here is granted! That this is an eternal danger I am not so sure. I can very well imagine today a shift to the opposite extreme: everything may become (and in some places is already becoming) so "corporate," so "socially oriented" that the essentially *personal* character of liturgical participation may be weakened. Thus, the historical and theological study of worship implies, of necessity, a serious consideration of liturgical piety, which at times can be *objectively* contradictory to liturgical norm.

⌘

On the problem of liturgical reform I can say this: it seems to me that the "anarchy" mentioned by Dom Botte and which permeates, to a degree, the liturgical scene in the West, is due primarily and precisely to a deep discrepancy between the "norms" as recovered by the Liturgical Movement and a new "liturgical piety" which claims the authority of Vatican II, yet is in many ways directly opposed to its liturgical directives. Whereas the Liturgical Movement, in its best representatives at least, was oriented towards a recovery of traditional elements of Christian *leitourgia*, elements which were obscured and even abolished for centuries, the "liturgical piety" which is behind modern "experimentations" and "anarchy" is inspired by an altogether different and indeed deeply *anti-traditional* set of aspirations. This obvious discrepancy between the "letter" of Vatican II and what is everywhere proclaimed to be its "spirit" and, thus, the justification for virtually every innovation, is a perplexing mystery for all watchers of the present Roman Catholic scene. What is important in the context of the present discussion, however, is precisely this phenomenon of "liturgical piety" which so often is fed at sources distinct from, if not opposed to, the objective norms and forms of the liturgy itself.

As for the need for a liturgical "reform" within the Orthodox Church, it seems to me that this concept must be qualified. For if anything is proved by the hectic reforms and changes in the West, it is that by themselves and in themselves they do not achieve what seems to be their goal. Liturgy is a living tradition, and surgery here is a wrong method. What we need above everything else is the understanding of that tradition, of the "essence" of liturgy. Once achieved it will lead — "organically" — to the necessary purifications and changes and this without any break of continuity, without any "crisis." In spite of a deeply rooted common opinion, liturgy always changes because it *lives.* One of the differences between the eastern and the western "mentalities" may be precisely in the western trust in planning and reforming from above. Yes, our liturgy, to be sure, carries with it many non-essential elements, many "archeological" remnants. But rather than denouncing them in the name of liturgical purity we must strive to discover and to help others to discover the *lex orandi,* which none of these accidental ingredients has managed to obscure. The time thus is not for an external liturgical reform but for a theology and piety drinking again from the eternal and unchanging sources of liturgical tradition.

3

Liturgical Reform: A Debate
Liturgical Theology and Liturgical Reform:
Some Questions

W Jardine Grisbrooke

Dom Botte's comments *On Liturgical Theology* and Father
Schmemann's *Brief Response* to them raise so many important
points that it is to be hoped that these distinguished liturgical
scholars will continue the exchange, and give us the benefit of their
thoughts on the subject at greater length.[1] In particular one would
welcome an expansion of Father Schmemann's reply to the questions Dom Botte puts to him in the last paragraph of the comments.

"The task of liturgical theology," writes Dom Botte,

> is then to recover the essential and to relegate the 'accessories' to their
> place. Does that imply a liturgical reform? This is what happened to
> Roman liturgy. A return to fundamental principles has resulted in a
> 'cleaning-up' as well as in new creativity. One has discovered that rigid
> forms were no longer adequate either to the essence of liturgy or the
> needs of the Christian people. Is a similar development possible and
> desirable within Byzantine liturgy? I am not competent to answer this
> question. The situation here is different from that of the Roman liturgy,
> where 'rubrics' had an absolute rigidity. The Eastern Church has always
> preserved a certain flexibility, but the freedom of a Byzantine celebrant
> is not limitless. Does the East need a reform? Is this the time for it? One
> understands perfectly well the hesitations and oppositions. The Roman
> reform was in preparation for half a century, but one can still ask

1. Published originally in *St Vladimir's Theological Quarterly*, 13, 1969, pp. 212–217.

whether things did not go too fast. The change was too abrupt and the
mania for experimentation has resulted here and there in anarchy. One
understands quite well that this example is a source for hesitation for
the easterners. Premature or one-sided reforms might do more harm
than good. And yet is the idea of a reform to be rejected altogether?
Ought not liturgical theology to prepare the fundamental principles of
a reform in continuity with, and respectful of, Tradition? To this
question Father Schmemann is more qualified to give an answer.

"As for the need for a liturgical 'reform' within the Orthodox
Church," replies Father Schmemann,

> it seems to me that this concept must be qualified. For if anything is
> proved by the hectic reforms and changes in the West, it is that by
> themselves and in themselves they do not achieve what seems to be their
> goal. Liturgy is a living tradition, and surgery here is a wrong method.
> What we need above everything else is the understanding of that
> tradition, of the 'essence' of liturgy. Once achieved it will lead—
> 'organically'—to the necessary purifications and changes and this with-
> out any break of continuity, without any 'crisis.' In spite of a deeply
> rooted common opinion, liturgy always changes because it *lives*. One
> of the differences between the eastern and western 'mentalities' may be
> precisely in the western trust in planning and reforming from above.
> Yes, our liturgy, to be sure, carries with it many non-essential elements,
> many 'archeological' remnants. But rather than denouncing them in
> the name of liturgical purity we must strive to discover the *lex orandi,*
> which none of these accidental ingredients has managed to obscure.
> The time thus is not for an external reform but for a theology and piety
> drinking again from the eternal and unchanging sources of liturgical
> tradition.

This last paragraph appears to me to lack the logic and lucidity
which usually mark whatever Father Schmemann writes. I agree
whole-heartedly with him that "if anything is proved by the hectic
reforms and changes in the West, it is that by themselves and in
themselves they do not achieve what seems to be their goal.
Liturgy is a living tradition ... What we need above everything
else is the understanding of that tradition, of the 'essence' of
liturgy." But I am unable to follow the rest of his argument.

By whom is this understanding of the liturgical tradition to be attained? Presumably, by the whole body of the faithful, clergy and laity alike. By what means is it to be attained? Apparently, by instruction — spiritual and intellectual — given by a minority already enlightened, or on its way to enlightenment; that is, one must assume, by liturgical scholars who have arrived at, or are in process of arriving at, an understanding of the tradition themselves, and, in turn, by those whom they teach: "we must strive to discover and to help others to discover the *lex orandi*, which none of these accidental ingredients has managed to obscure."

Will not the liturgically educated parish priest — and he it is on whom, in practice, the burden of this task will largely fall — trying to help his congregation in this way, find at once that these "accidental ingredients" *have* managed to "obscure" the *lex orandi*? If they have not, why has there been such a loss of understanding, why is it necessary to rediscover it?

Is the *lex orandi* itself so feeble a thing that understanding of it, or lack of such understanding depends entirely on influences external to it? If this is so, then "organic" recovery of a proper understanding of it is out of the question: how can such a recovery be attained except by "external liturgical reform?" If it is not so, how can the recovery be attained without putting right what has gone wrong in the *lex orandi* itself? And how, then, can we talk of the "*unchanging* sources of liturgical tradition"? Or are the sources of liturgical tradition external to the *lex orandi*, and if so precisely what are they, and what is the relationship of the *lex orandi* to them? Is it possible to recover a truly liturgical piety without eliminating from the liturgy itself the distortions which the loss of such a piety since the high middle ages has imported into it? If it is not, then "external liturgical reform" in another sense is necessary, is it not? And if it is possible, can we speak any longer of a *lex orandi* at all? Is not this to reduce the liturgy itself to an arbitrary "protocol of public relations with God," to use Dom Botte's perceptive phrase? What are "liturgical theology" and "liturgical piety" if not a theology and a piety founded on the liturgy? And how can they be recovered or restored except the integrity of the liturgy itself be recovered or restored? Of course the two processes go hand in hand, but surely it must be a two-way traffic?

To take a simple example: suppose a parish priest is concerned to give his people a real understanding of the significance of the so-called "little entrance" — a subject on which Father Schmemann has elsewhere written perceptively and illuminatingly. How can he do so without pointing out the deficiencies of the present form of it — "denouncing them in the name of liturgical purity"? How can he do that without realizing, and leading others to realize, that the historical development here has served to obscure the *lex orandi* to such an extent that it is almost invisible? And having acquired a real, and spiritually valuable, understanding of it, are he and his people to be satisfied, when actually worshipping, with the meaningless decadent form of it?

No, apparently not, but they do not need to do anything about seeking a change, for such a change will come about, not by way of an "external liturgical reform" consequent upon "planning and reforming from above," but "organically." Understanding of the *lex orandi* "will lead — 'organically' — to the necessary purifications and changes and this without any break of continuity," without any 'crisis.' "

What exactly does this mean? It sounds impressive, but what does it *mean*, what would it mean in practice? Is it possible for a change not to be a change? If it is not, how can it be other than a "break of continuity" in some sense and to some extent? If this is not what Father Schmemann means by a "break of continuity," what does he mean by it? Does he mean liturgical reform of so drastic a kind and so great an extent as to amount to a complete upheaval of the *lex orandi?* If so, what does he envisage happening? Does he mean liturgical reform which some people will *suppose* to be complete upheaval? If so, is it not almost inevitable that *any* measure of reform will be regarded in that way in some quarters? And will not that inevitably produce some kind, and some measure, of "crisis," no matter when, by whom, or in what way, the reform is initiated or carried out?

And when, by whom, and in what way, *is* it to be initiated and carried out? Not by "planning and reforming from above," but "organically." I ask again, what exactly does "organically" mean, then? Does it mean that one morning a whole congregation will wake up, find its understanding of the liturgical tradition has come to maturity overnight, and automatically, without any discussion, without any planning, go to church and "do" the liturgy entirely differently from the way in which they did it last week? Is liturgical change to wait until every single member of a parish has come to see the need for it? Presumably not, for in that case neither this nor anything else would ever happen: such a situation is unlikely in the extreme. But if not, then would not such changes, decided on by the parish priest and parish council, even if at the desire of the majority of the congregation, be evidently due in practice — and certainly in the eyes of the dissenters — to "planning and reforming from above" to some extent?

Again, by whose authority are these changes to be made? Are they to be made in any church whose priest and people have come to see them as necessary or desirable, without consulting any higher authority? That would produce liturgical anarchy indeed. It would also produce canonical anarchy, of which there is more than enough already. If such changes are to be made without episcopal and synodical authority, just what kind of an "organism" is this Church? But perhaps they are to be made only with this authority, at one level or another. Then the same questions recur. Is a whole diocese, or province, or even a whole autocephalous church, going to wake up one morning convinced of the need for changes, and, moreover, in complete instinctive agreement as to what changes are necessary, and how to carry them out

in practice? Are such changes to wait until every one of the
faithful within its jurisdiction is convinced of the need for them?
If the answer to these questions is "no" — and to answer them
affirmatively would be ridiculously unrealistic — then presumably the changes are to be made, and their details laid down, by
episcopal and synodical authority. And that would involve "planning and reforming from above," would it not? *Somebody* "below"
would be bound to disagree with them, in one way or another: to
suppose otherwise is to ignore human nature.

Is not Father Schmemann's position really determined by the
fear that if the force of reform is once let loose it will go astray, and
end up by destroying rather than renewing the *lex orandi* and a
truly liturgical piety based upon it? It certainly seems so, in the
light of what he writes about the current reforms in the Roman
Catholic Church:

> Whereas the Liturgical Movement, in its best representatives at least,
> was oriented towards a recovery of traditional elements of Christian
> *leitourgia*, elements which were obscured and even abolished for cen-
> turies, the "liturgical piety" which is behind modern "experimenta-
> tions" and "anarchy" is inspired by an altogether different and indeed
> deeply *anti-traditional* set of aspirations.

This is true, although it is by no means the whole truth. But
insofar as it is true, *why* is it? *Why* has this situation come about?
Dom Botte writes: "One understands perfectly the hesitations
and oppositions. The Roman reform was in preparation for half a
century, but one can still ask whether things did not go too fast."
One can indeed, and one should. But one should also ask whether
for a long time they did not go too slow, and whether this is not a
major factor in the situation, whether this is not the real reason
why in the event "the change was too abrupt and the mania for
experimentation has resulted here and there in anarchy." Is not
this the real danger of which Father Schmemann should be afraid?
Is not *this* the situation which Father Schmemann should be
concerned to avert? The "reform in continuity with, and respect-

ful of, Tradition" of which the theologians and liturgists of the liturgical movement laid the foundations was held back so long that now it has been confused and to some extent vitiated by the "altogether different and indeed deeply anti-traditional set of aspirations" of which Father Schmemann speaks. The organic impulse of the living tradition to change in accord with its own nature was throttled for so long that now the changes are being made under the influence of external factors not in accord with its nature. Had a truly traditional reform been undertaken earlier, and had had time to come to fruition, these anti-traditional aspirations might never have arisen, let alone become so strong and powerful. Is not *this* the important and urgent lesson which the Orthodox Church should learn from the present confusion in the Roman Catholic Church?

"Liturgy," says Father Schmemann, "is a living tradition, and surgery here is a wrong method." Is it? Surgery is never desirable, never comfortable: but are there not times when it is necessary — precisely in order to ensure that the patient goes on living? And if the liturgical tradition of the Orthodox Church is in as grave a condition as Father Schmemann has himself diagnosed elsewhere, is not this clearly such a time?

多   多   多

Liturgical Theology, Theology of Liturgy, and Liturgical Reform

Alexander Schmemann

I am very thankful to W Jardine Grisbrooke for his comments and questions, but I am not sure my answer will satisfy him.[2] For it seems to me that his remarks, as well as those by Dom Botte, are based on a rather serious misunderstanding of some of my main "theses" and I do not know whether this misunderstanding has its roots in the defects of my presentation or in some deeper disagreement on the very nature of liturgical theology. In the first case my answer may clarify the issue, in the second it will probably deepen the disagreement.

W J Grisbrooke, following in this Dom Botte, assumes that for me "the task of liturgical theology is to recover the essential and to relegate the 'accessories' to their place" and thus to prepare grounds for a liturgical reform that would restore the "essence" of the liturgy. If this assumption were true W J Grisbrooke would be perfectly right, of course, in denouncing my "lack of logic and lucidity" and my, then clearly irresponsible, reluctance to admit the urgent need for a liturgical reform.

The fact, however, is that such is *not* my concept of liturgical theology and that therefore my approach to the complex question of a liturgical reform is not necessarily the result of a "lack of logic." What I tried to say in my book, and also in some other writings, is that the "essence" of the liturgy or *lex orandi* is ultimately nothing else but the Church's faith itself or, better to say, the manifestation, communication and fulfillment of that faith. It is in this sense that one must understand, it seems to me,

2. This reply to W. Jardine Grisbrooke appeared in the same issue of *St Vladimir's Theological Quarterly*, 13, 1969, pp. 217-224.

the famous dictum *lex orandi est lex credendi.* It does not imply a reduction of the faith to liturgy or cult, as was the case in the mystery cults in which faith was aimed at cult itself, had its saving power as its object. Nor does it mean a confusion between faith and liturgy as in the case of the liturgical piety in which the "liturgical experience," the experience of the "sacred," simply replaces faith and makes one indifferent to its "doctrinal" content. Nor finally does it indicate a separation of faith and liturgy into two distinct "essences" whose content and meaning are to be grasped by two different and independent means of investigation, as in modern theology in which the study of liturgy constitutes a special area or discipline: "liturgiology." What it means is that the Church's *leitourgia,* a term incidentally much more comprehensive and adequate than "worship" or "cult," is the full and adequate "epiphany" — expression, manifestation, fulfillment of that in which the church believes, or what constitutes her faith. It implies an organic and essential interdependence in which one element, the faith, although source and cause of the other, the liturgy, essentially needs the other as its own self-understanding and self-fulfillment. It is, to be sure, faith that gives birth to, and "shapes," liturgy, but it is liturgy, that by fulfilling and expressing faith, "bears testimony" to faith and becomes thus its true and adequate expression and norm: *lex orandi est lex credendi.*

But then liturgical theology — and I cannot overemphasize this — is *not* that part of theology, that "discipline," which deals with liturgy "in itself," has liturgy as its specific "object," but, first of all and above everything else, the attempt to grasp the "theology" as revealed in and through liturgy. There is, I maintain, a radical and indeed irreducible difference between these two approaches to liturgical theology whose task then obviously depends on whether one opts for one or the other.

In the first approach, which both Dom Botte and W J Grisbrooke think and assume is mine, one indeed looks for the specific "essence" of the liturgy as a whole or of any one of its basic elements: sacraments, Divine Office, cycles of worship, etc. Here liturgical theology is understood primarily and in fact exclusively, as *theology of liturgy*, as search for a consistent theology of worship with which, once it is formulated, the liturgy must "comply" by means of a liturgical reform if necessary.

At this point I can only emphatically state that the rejection of this approach, the certitude that it is wrong and harmful for both liturgy and theology is without any exaggeration the primary motivation of my work. In the approach which I advocate by every line I ever wrote, the question addressed by liturgical theology to liturgy and to the entire liturgical tradition is not about liturgy but about "theology," i.e. about the faith of the Church as expressed, communicated and preserved by the liturgy. Here liturgy is viewed as the *locus theologicus par excellence* because it is its very function, its *leitourgia* in the original meaning of that word, to manifest and to fulfill the Church's faith and to manifest it not partially, not "discursively," but as living totality and catholic experience. And it is because liturgy is that living totality and that catholic experience by the Church of her own faith that it is the very *source* of theology, the condition that makes it *possible*. For if theology, as the Orthodox Church maintains, is not a mere sequence of more or less individual interpretations of this or that "doctrine" in the light and thought forms of this or that "culture" and "situation," but the attempt to express Truth itself, to find words adequate to the mind and experience of the Church, then it must of necessity have its source where the faith, the mind, and the experience of the Church have their living focus and expression, where faith in both essential meanings of that word, as Truth revealed and given, and as Truth accepted and "lived," has its *epiphany*, and that is precisely the function of the *leitourgia*.

It must be clear by now that the tragedy which I denounce and deplore consists not in any particular "defect" of the liturgy —

and God knows that there have been many such defects at all times — but in something much deeper: the *divorce between liturgy, theology, and piety*, a divorce which characterizes the post-patristic period of the history of our Church and which has altered — not the faith and not too much the liturgy — theology and piety. In other terms, the crisis which I try to analyze is the crisis not of liturgy but of its *understanding* — be it in the "key" of post-patristic theology or in that of a rather recent, but assumed to be traditional, liturgical piety. And precisely because the roots of the crisis are theological and spiritual rather than liturgical, no liturgical reform can by itself and in itself solve it.

Take for example the organic, and for the early Church self-evident, connection and interdependence within the *lex orandi*, of the Lord's Day, the Eucharist and the *Ecclesia* (the coming together of the faithful as "church"). If it was self-evident and so central as to have, in fact, shaped the liturgical tradition of the Church, it is because it was both the expression and the fulfillment of something equally central and essential in the Church's faith: the unity and interdependence in that faith of the cosmological, eschatological, and ecclesiological "experiences." It was born out of the Christian vision and experience of the World, the Church, and the Kingdom, of their fundamental relationship to one another. Now, it is clear that on the one hand, this connection still exists *liturgically*, but it is equally clear that on the other hand, it is neither understood nor experienced in the way it was understood and experienced in the early Church. Why? Because a certain theology and a certain piety shaped by that theology, by imposing their own categories and their own approach changed our understanding of the liturgy and our experience of it. In this particular case they did it by depriving this "connection" of its cosmological, eschatological and ecclesiological meaning and connotations. The connection itself remained a part of the *lex orandi* but it ceased to be related in any way to the *lex credendi*, was no longer regarded as a theological *datum* and no theologian has even

bothered to mention it as having any theological significance, as
revealing anything about the Church's "experience" of herself, the
World, and the Kingdom of God. Thus the Lord's Day became
simply the Christian form of Sabbath, the Eucharist one "means
of grace" among many and the Church — an institution with
sacraments but no longer sacramental in her very nature and
"constitution." But then one may ask: what liturgical, i.e., external, reform could possibly restore that experience, return its original meaning to that "connection"? It is still here, with us. It is still
the norm and yet we do not see it. It resounds in every word of
eucharistic celebration — yet we do not hear it. It is as if someone
imposed on our eyes glasses which make us blind to the obvious,
and on our ears hearing aids that make us deaf to the most
explicit.

The real problem then is not that of "liturgical reforms" but,
first of all, of the much needed "reconciliation" and mutual
reintegration of liturgy, theology and piety. Here, however, I
must confess my pessimism. I do not see in Orthodox theology
and in general in the Orthodox Church even a recognition of that
problem and it is clear to me that unless a problem is recognized
its solution is either impossible or there will be a wrong solution.
Thus, for example, I do not expect great results from the much
talked about "return to the Fathers" in which some see the pana-
cea against all evils. For, in my opinion, it all depends on *how* one
"returns" to the Fathers. It is my impression that with a few
exceptions, the "patristic revival" remains locked within the old
western approach to theology, is a return much more to patristic
texts than to the *mind* of the Fathers, as if these patristic texts were
self-sufficient and self-explanatory. It is indeed the "original sin"
of the entire western theological development that it made "texts"
the only *loci theologici*, the extrinsic "authorities" of theology,
disconnecting theology from its living source: liturgy and spirituality.

The paradox of some of contemporary Orthodox theology is that one may denounce — in the name of the Fathers — all kinds of western heresies while remaining at the same time profoundly "western" as to the basic presuppositions and the very nature of theology. One may produce more or less interesting, more or less scholarly monographs on the patristic "idea" or "doctrine" of this or that, and give the impression that the Fathers were primarily "thinkers" who, as today's theologians, worked exclusively on "biblical texts" and "philosophical concepts." What this approach ignores is precisely the ecclesiological and liturgical context of patristic thought. And it ignores it — and here is the crux of the matter — because by western scholarly principles, techniques, and criteria adopted long ago by our theologians as the only valid ones — this context is not immediately perceivable. The Fathers very seldom explicitly refer to it, their "texts" do not mention it and the patristic scholar respectful of texts and of "evidence" cashable in the form of "footnotes" is, in virtue of his very method, unable to perceive it. There are theologians extremely well read in patristics and utterly convinced of their own traditionalism who, for example, denounce as non-patristic and non-traditional the idea of the organic connection and interdependence between ecclesiology and Eucharist because the "texts" do not formally evidence this idea. And of course if theological inquiry is *a priori* limited to "texts" — be they scriptural, patristic or even liturgical — these theologians are right. But the real meaning of this *argumentum a silentio* is different. For the Fathers this connection is not something to be theologically established, defined and proved, but the source making theology itself possible. They rarely speak of the Church and of liturgy in explicit terms because for them they are not an "object" of theology but its ontological foundation, the epiphany, the reality, the self-evidence of that to which then in their writings they "bear testimony." And this is exactly what makes them Fathers, i.e. witnesses of the "mind" of the Church, exponents of her catholic "experience." Disconnected from that source and that context, patristic "texts" just as biblical texts, can be interpreted in many ways, to prove almost anything. And they remain, at best, "ideas" and "doctrines," confined to academic quarters but as alienated from the real life of the Church as the old westernized theology of seminary manuals. Here, as in the case of the *lex orandi,* one may very well look without seeing and listen without hearing. To put it in today's fashionable terms, the theological enterprise depends on "hermeneutics," the latter being precisely the fundamental question of context and semantics. My contention is that for Orthodox theology, essentially different in this from western theology, the *sui generis* hermeneutical foundation is to be found in the *lex orandi*: the epiphany and the experience by the Church of herself and of her faith. This is what we mean when we state, in accordance with our Tradition, that the scripture is interpreted "by the Church," and that the Fathers are witnesses of the catholic faith of the Church. And as long, therefore, as this Orthodox "hermeneutics" is not acknowledged, rediscovered and practiced, the scrutiny of the most traditional "texts" will, alas, remain as irrelevant for our liturgical situation as in the past.

Even less hope do I place in all kinds of liturgical "revivals" which periodically shake up the complacency of ecclesiastical "establishments" and inevitably lead to discussions about liturgical reforms. For a liturgical reform (the need for which incidentally I do not deny) must have a rationale, a consistent set of presuppositions and goals, and this rationale, as I keep repeating, can only be found in the *lex orandi* and in the organic relationship to the *lex credendi*. But I do not detect even the slightest interest in such a rationale among those — and they are many — who have the liturgy in the center of their preoccupations. We find, on the one hand, a romantic and nostalgic pathos of liturgical restoration, a genuine fixation on rubrics and rules, but without any interest in the relation they may or may not have to the faith of the Church. No wonder that in this approach the objects and selected goals of such a restoration vary almost *ad infinitum*. There are fanatics of Russian liturgical piety — ancient or modern, and those of the Greek style, there are those for whom everything depends on the restoration of a particular "chant" or on maintaining "little litanies" as prescribed by the rubrics. When people of this brand discover, for example, that in the Russian (and relatively recent) practice the Royal Doors were closed during the eucharistic canon, they denounce those who advocate that they be open as heretics and modernists. We find, on the other hand, the opposite trend: those obsessed with making liturgy more "understandable," "relevant," and "closer to the people." Here the set of fixations and of means considered as immediate panaceas is exactly an opposite one: remove the iconostasis, read all prayers aloud, shorten the services, abolish everything which is not related to "togetherness," introduce congregational singing, translate everything into the most popular and plain kind of English, fight any "ethnic" custom, etc. But whatever the approach, no meaningful discussion of it is possible because in all of them any interest in precisely the *meaning* of the liturgy as a whole, of the *lex orandi* in its relationship to the *lex credendi* is absent, because the liturgy is viewed as an end in itself and not as the "epiphany" of the Church's faith, of her experience in Christ of herself, the World and the Kingdom.

Take, for example, today's polarization within the Church on the question of "frequent communion." It is indeed a strange debate in which both sides, i.e. those who advocate "frequent" communion and those who oppose it, never refer to the only important question which, paradoxically as it may sound, is — "What is communion?" or rather — "To *what* and to *whom* is it communion?" I say "paradoxically" because both sides consider this question as perfectly clear, not even a question. They would answer: to the Body of Christ, to the "Holy Mysteries." Yet it is the whole point that the different practices of communion, which can all be argued for as being "traditional," were in the last analysis the result of different "theologies" and "pieties," of different ways of looking at Eucharist and at the Church herself, ways which all need to be re-examined in the light of the genuine *lex orandi*. Thus, those who oppose "frequent" communion are not necessarily less "pious" than those who advocate it, just as the latter are not necessarily advocating it for the right reasons. The tragedy of all these debates on the liturgy is that they remain locked within the categories of a "liturgical piety" which is itself the outcome of the divorce between liturgy, theology and piety, a divorce which I have mentioned above. And as long as this liturgical piety dominates and shapes these debates the very notion of liturgical reform may be not only useless but even dangerous.

Indeed, the sad lesson of the present liturgical confusion in the West must not be lost on us. This confusion, especially in the Roman Church, is due precisely to the absence of a clear and consistent rationale for liturgical reform. It is truly sad that some fifty years of constructive work within the Liturgical Movement were simply swept away by a hasty acceptance of such principles as the famous "relevance," or "urgent needs of modern society," "the celebration of life," or "social justice." The result is a disintegration of liturgy and this in spite of some excellent ideas and a great deal of liturgical competence.

Finally one may ask: but what do you propose, what do you want? To this I will answer without much hope, I confess, of being heard and understood: we need *liturgical theology*, viewed not as a theology of worship and not as a reduction of theology to liturgy, but as a slow and patient bringing together of that which was for too long a time and because of many factors broken and isolated — liturgy, theology and piety, their reintegration within one fundamental vision. In this sense liturgical theology is an illegitimate child of a broken family. It exists, or maybe I should say it ought to exist, only because theology ceased to seek in the *lex orandi* its source and food, because liturgy ceased to be conducive to theology. We must learn — and it is not easy — to ask of the liturgy the right questions and for this we must rediscover — and again it is not easy — the genuine *lex orandi* of the Church. And above all we must start questioning the very spirit, organization, and method of our theology and the entire educational process which we have uncritically, blindly, accepted from the post-Tridentine West and which we present today as traditional and Orthodox. It may be consistent with some Western theological presuppositions to split theology into a number of virtually autonomous and self sufficient "departments" or "disciplines" — Biblical Theology, Systematic Theology, Patristics, Liturgy, Canon Law. In the Orthodox Church it not only ultimately leads nowhere, but, what is worse, distorts in a very subtle way the theological work itself, imposing on it questions, categories and problems simply alien to the "mind" of the Church.

All this, I repeat, not only is not in sight but no one seems to understand the real scope of the problem. It seems to me sometimes that the genuine *secularists* are not the "secular" people of our time whom we constantly chide and condemn for their secularism, but many of our professional theologians, clergymen, and "pious" laity. The "secular" man shows at least signs of discontent with his secularism, is more and more nostalgic of a sacred depth and *wholeness.* Only we seem to accept, without even noticing it, the brokenness of our Christian vision and experience into neat and unrelated compartments, to accept as normal a legalized and institutionalized divorce within which neither theology nor liturgy can truly be the victory which overcomes the world ... But for the time being the voice of those who denounce it and call for a *reintegration* — such being exactly the task of liturgical theology — is likely to remain *vox clamans in deserto.*

4

Liturgy and Theology

I

The time has come for a deep re-evaluation of the relationship between theology and liturgy.[1] My purpose in this paper is to explain the reasons for that affirmation, and to indicate, be it only tentatively, its meaning for the Orthodox theological enterprise as a whole, and also for the liturgical problems whose existence and urgency are acknowledged today by nearly everyone.

Very few people, I am sure, would deny that the Orthodox Church is in a state of crisis; yet very few also are those, it seems to me, who realize that at the bottom of this crisis, as one of its main sources, lies the double crisis of theology and liturgy.

A crisis of theology! Is it not obvious indeed that the confusion and the divisions we witness today on virtually every level of the Church's life — the canonical, the administrative, the educational, the "ecumenical" — are rooted, first of all, in the absence of commonly accepted and acknowledged terms of reference or criteria which normally are to be supplied precisely by theology? Contemporary Orthodox theology is unable to supply such norms because it is itself "broken." It is characterized, on the one hand, by an unhealthy pluralism and, on the other hand, by a peculiar inability to communicate with the "real" Church. I call this pluralism unhealthy because there can exist and there existed in the past a healthy theological pluralism perfectly compatible with a fundamental unity. For example, there certainly were

1. Appeared originally in *The Greek Orthodox Theological Review*, 17, 1972, pp. 86–100.

substantial differences among the Fathers, but they did not break
the basic unity of a common experience and vision. Today, however, it is precisely such common vision that seems to be lacking.
To put it somewhat sharply, Orthodox theologians do not seem to
understand one another, so different are the respective "keys" in
which they approach the same problems, so opposed to one
another their basic presuppositions and thought forms. This leads
either to meaningless polemics — for to be meaningful polemics
would require a minimum of agreement as to the basic terms of
reference — polemics in which the awesome word "heresy" is
used more and more often without any discrimination, or to a
kind of "peaceful coexistence" of theological orientations mutually ignoring one another.

Whatever its "key" or orientation, this theology moreover
seems deeply alienated from the Church, from her real life and
needs. Although taught in official ecclesiastical schools, its impact
on students usually evaporates on the day of graduation. It is
viewed as an intellectual abstraction nowhere to be really applied;
as an intellectual game which the people of God — clergy and
laity — simply ignore. In our Church today, professional theologians constitute a kind of *Lumpenproletariat* and, what is even
more tragic, seem to be reconciled to this status. Theology is no
longer the conscience and the consciousness of the Church, her
reflection on herself and on her problems. It has ceased to be
pastoral in the sense of providing the Church with essential and
saving norms; and it has also ceased to be *mystical* in the sense of
communicating to the people of God the knowledge of God
which is the very content of life eternal. A theology alienated from
the Church, and a Church alienated from theology; such is the
first dimension of today's crisis.

II

The situation of the liturgy is not much better. It has, to be sure, remained the focus, the "holy of holies" of the Church's life; it is still the main — one almost should say the exclusive — occupation of the Church. Yet a deeper analysis would reveal here also a very serious crisis which cannot be resolved by hasty and superficial liturgical reforms advocated by many today. A first aspect of this crisis is the growing nominalism of the liturgical life and practice. In spite of its apparent conservatism and even archaism, this practice is hardly expressive of the genuine *lex orandi* of the Church. Entire and essential strata of liturgical tradition, while faithfully preserved in liturgical books, are little by little disappearing from practice or then preserved symbolically and transformed beyond recognition. Eucharist and the sacraments, liturgical seasons and the celebration of feasts, rites of blessing and sanctification of life — everywhere one finds the same pattern: a "selection" of certain elements, a rejection of others; a selection, however, based not on the principles of the *lex orandi* itself but on considerations totally alien to it. If the average church-goer may not notice this rapid erosion of Orthodox worship, the specialist cannot help being worried by the growing discrepancy between the demands of tradition on the one hand, and the nominalism and minimalism of the liturgical piety and practice on the other hand.

What is more serious, however, is the fact that the liturgy — central as it may be within the activities of the Church — has ceased to be connected with virtually all other aspects of the Church's life; to inform, shape and guide the ecclesiastical consciousness as well as the "worldview" of the Christian community. One may be deeply attached to the "ancient and colorful rites" of Byzantium or Russia, see in them precious relics of a cherished past, be a liturgical "conservative"; and, at the same time, completely fail to see in them, in the totality of the Church's *leitourgia*,

an all-embracing vision of life, a power meant to judge, inform
and transform the whole of existence, a "philosophy of life"
shaping and challenging all our ideas, attitudes and actions. As in
the case of theology, one can speak of an alienation of liturgy from
life, be it the life of the Church or the life of a Christian individual. Liturgy is confined to the temple, but beyond its sacred
enclave it has no impact, no power. All other ecclesiastical activities — in a parish, a diocese, a local church — are based more and
more on purely secular presuppositions and logics, as are also the
various "philosophies of life" adopted by professed Christians.
Liturgy is neither explained nor understood as having anything to
do with "life"; as, above all, an *icon* of that new life which is to
challenge and renew the "old life" in us and around us. A liturgical pietism fed by sentimental and pseudo-symbolical explanations of liturgical rites results, in fact, in a growing and
all-pervading secularism. Having become in the mind of the
faithful something "sacred" *per se*, liturgy makes even more "profane" the real life which begins beyond the sacred doors of the
temple.

This double crisis — of theology and liturgy — is, I submit,
the real source of the general crisis which faces our Church today,
and which must shape our agenda, if theology is for us more than
a quiet "academic" activity; if we understand it as our specific
charism and ministry within the Body of Christ. A crisis is always
a divorce, a discrepancy, between the foundations and the life
which is supposed to be based on these foundations; it is life
drifting away from its own foundations. The Church's life has
always been rooted in the *lex credendi*, the rule of faith, theology
in the deepest sense of the word; and on the *lex orandi*, her rule of
worship, the *leitourgia* which always "makes her what she is": the
Body of Christ and the Temple of the Holy Spirit. Today, however, there is developing rapidly a dangerous alienation of the
"real" Church from these two sources of her life. Such is our
situation: such is the crisis whose challenge is upon us — whether

we acknowledge it or not. To understand it in its deep causes is, therefore, the first and necessary step. Our question thus must be: why and how did it occur?

III

I have no doubts as to the answer. If today both theology and liturgy have ceased, at least to a substantial degree, to perform within the Church the function which is theirs, thus provoking a deep crisis, it is because at first they have been divorced from one another; because the *lex credendi* has been alienated from the *lex orandi*. When did this happen? During that post-patristic "western captivity" of Orthodox theology which in my opinion constitutes one of the main tragedies on the historical path of Eastern Orthodoxy. This "western captivity" consisted primarily in what Fr Florovsky so aptly termed the "pseudomorphosis" of the eastern theological mind — the adoption by it of western thought forms and categories, of the western understanding of the very nature, structure, and method of theology. And the first, and indeed the most fateful, result of that "pseudomorphosis" was precisely a mutual alienation from one another of the *lex credendi* and the *lex orandi*.

The purpose of theology is an orderly and consistent presentation, explication and defense of the Church's faith. This faith is thus both its source and its "object," and the entire structure and method of theology depend therefore on how one understands the nature of its relationship to that "source," i.e., to the faith of the Church. It is at this point that a radical difference exists or, better to say, existed between the East and the West; a difference later obscured, if not entirely removed, by the "western captivity" of eastern theology. It was in the West at first, and for reasons inherent to the western religious and intellectual development, that the "source" of theology, i.e., the Church's faith, began to be identified with a specific number of "data," mainly texts —

scriptural, patristic, conciliar — which as *loci theologici* were to
supply the theological speculation with its subject matter and
criteria. With the entire theological enterprise in the West being
aimed primarily at constructing an *objective* or *scientific* theology,
it was both natural and essential for it to establish itself on an
equally objective and clearly defined foundation. Hence, the identification of faith, in theological terms, with "propositions"; hence
also the rejection from the theological process of any reference to
or dependence upon *experience*.

Yet it is precisely faith *as experience*, the total and living experience of the Church, that constitutes the source and the context of
theology in the East, of that theology at least which characterized
the patristic age. It is "description" more than "definition" for it
is, above all, a search for words and concepts adequate to and
expressive of the living experience of the Church; for a *reality* and
not "propositions." It is itself a part and a fruit of that experience,
and it is in this sense that Vladimir Lossky calls it "mystical
theology." Its criteria lie not in formal and, therefore, autonomous "authorities," but in its adequacy to and consistency with
the inner life and experience of the Church. This understanding
of theology stems from the very nature of its "source," i.e., the
faith of the Church. For the faith which founds the Church and
by which she lives is not a mere assent to a "doctrine," but her
living relationship to certain events: the Life, Death, Resurrection
and Glorification of Jesus Christ, His Ascension to heaven, the
descent of the Holy Spirit on the "last and great day of Pentecost"
— a relationship which makes her a constant "witness" and
"participant" of these events, of their saving, redeeming, life-giving and life-transfiguring reality. She has indeed no other experience but the experience of these events; no other life but the "new
life" they always generate and communicate. Her faith thus is not
only not detachable from her experience, but is indeed that experience itself — the experience of that "which we have heard,
which we have seen with our eyes, which we have looked upon

and touched with our hands," (1 Jn 1:1). For none of these events can be known, in the rational meaning of that word, nor even believed in outside the experience which reveals their reality and makes us "witness to these things." But then theology cannot be anything else but the "description" of that experience, its revelation in human words and concepts. The Church is not an institution that keeps certain divinely revealed "doctrines" and "teachings" about this or that event of the past, but the very *epiphany* of these events themselves. And she can teach about them because, first of all, she knows them; because she is the experience of their reality. Her faith as teaching and theology is rooted in her faith as experience. Her *lex credendi* is revealed in her life.

IV

I can now come to the main thesis of this paper: this *experience* of the Church is primarily the experience given and received in the Church's *leitourgia* — in her *lex orandi*. That today we must defend and prove this thesis is indeed the most bitter result of the "pseudomorphosis" of our theology mentioned above. What centuries of "western captivity" did was not only alter the theological "mind" but, by the same token, tragically narrow and obscure the very concept and experience of liturgy, of its place and function within the life of the Church. To put it abruptly: the liturgy ceased to be viewed and experienced as the *epiphany* of the Church's faith, as the reality of her experience as Church and, therefore, as the source of her theology.

If indeed liturgy remained and still remains at the center of the Church's life and activity, if it changed very little as to its form and content, it acquired a "coefficient"; began to be comprehended and experienced in a "key" substantially different from those of the earlier patristic age. It suffices to consult any post-patristic manual of dogmatics to find the sacraments, for example, treated in the chapters devoted to "means of grace" and nowhere else, as if they had nothing to do with the faith itself, the structure of the Church or knowledge of God. As to the liturgical tradition in its totality, it has in the same manuals no place whatsoever; the implication being obviously that it belongs to the area of *cult* or *piety*, essentially different from that of dogma and theology. It is precisely this reduction of the liturgy, or the *lex orandi*, to "cult," its understanding exclusively in cultic categories, that reveals the new coefficient, is the new key of both liturgical practice and liturgical piety, and a major obstacle to its theological understanding, to a living communication between liturgy and theology.

In the early Church, however—and I have stressed it elsewhere —even the term *leitourgia* was not, as it is today, a mere synonym of *cult*. It was applied indeed to all those ministries and offices within the Church in which she manifested and fulfilled her nature and vocation; it had primarily ecclesiological and not cultic connotations. And the very fact that subsequently it was identified especially with "Divine Liturgy," the central act of Christian cult, reveals above all the peculiar character, the uniqueness of that cult itself, of its place and function within the Church. From the very beginning, this unique function was precisely to "make the Church what she is" — the witness and the participant of the saving *event* of Christ, of the new life in the Holy Spirit, of the presence in "this world" of the Kingdom to come.

To baptize by water and spirit in the likeness of Christ's Death and Resurrection; to "come together as Church" on the Lord's Day, to hear His Word and "to eat and drink at His table in His Kingdom"; to relate — through the "liturgy of time" — all time, all cosmos — its time, matter and life — as a sacramental icon of Christ who is to "fill all things with Himself": all this was not understood as mere "cultic acts" but, above all, as the fulfillment by the Church of her very nature, of her cosmic and eschatological calling.

Here is the essential point: in the early patristic Church, ecclesiology is cosmic and eschatological. The Church is the mystery of the new creation and she is the mystery of the Kingdom. It has often been said that there is no ecclesiology, in the modern sense of this word, in the writings of the Fathers. The reason for that, however, is not a lack of interest in the Church, but their understanding and experience of the Church as the new life of the new creation and the presence, the "*parousia,*" of the Kingdom. Their attention is not focused on the "institution" because the very nature and purpose of that institution is not to exist "in itself" but to be the "sacrament," the *epiphany* of the new creation. In this sense, their whole theology is ecclesiological for it has the Church, the experience of the new life, the communion of the Holy Spirit as its source and context. From this point of view the post-Tridentine *De Ecclesia*, mother and pattern of all modern ecclesiology both western and eastern, is indeed a downfall of patristic ecclesiology; for it focuses the attention almost exclusively on the "institution," and away from its cosmic and eschatological nature and goal. It makes "institution" a kind of end in itself, and in doing this, in apparently exalting the Church, it, in fact, tragically mutilates her; making her as we see it today more and more "irrelevant" for the world, less and less "expressive" of the Kingdom of God.

What is important for us at this point is the relationship between this cosmic and eschatological nature of the Church and her *leitourgia*. For it is precisely in and through her liturgy — this being the latter's specific and unique "function" — that the Church is *informed* of her cosmic and eschatological vocation, *receives* the power to fulfill it and thus truly *becomes* "what she is" — the sacrament, in Christ, of the new creation; the sacrament, in Christ, of the Kingdom. In this sense the liturgy is indeed "means of grace," not in the narrow and individualistic meaning given this term in post-patristic theology, but in the all-embracing meaning, as means of always making the Church what she is — a

realm of grace, of communion with God, of new knowledge and
new life. The liturgy of the Church is cosmic and eschatological
because the Church is cosmic and eschatological; but the Church
would not have been cosmic and eschatological had she not been
given, as the very source and constitution of her life and faith, the
experience of the new creation, the experience and *vision* of the
Kingdom which is to come. And this is precisely the *leitourgia* of
the Church's cult, the function which makes it the source and
indeed the very *possibility* of theology.

V

The theological and liturgical tragedy of the post-patristic age is
that the Church's cult was deprived of its liturgical function and
reduced to cultic categories alone. This means more precisely that
the theological mind as well as piety ceased to see in it, to
experience it, as the very epiphany of the cosmic and eschatological "content" of the Church's faith and thus of the Church
herself. Yet once detached from this, its essential cosmic and
eschatological content, the liturgy of the Church, her *lex orandi*,
simply cannot be properly "heard" and understood; then inevitably a deterioration of theology and piety begins; their own
"pseudomorphosis" takes place — the more dangerous because of
its taking place not in the forms of the liturgy, but in their inner
comprehension and usage by the faithful. Paradoxical as it may
seem, it is very often the liturgical "conservative," the passionate
lover of rubrics and externals, the amateur of "ancient and colorful" rites who is most hopelessly blind to the true meaning of
these very rites, to the "Truth and Spirit" which gave them birth
and of which they are both manifestation and gift.

Signs and symptoms of that deterioration are too many to be
enumerated even here; a few, however, ought to be mentioned.
Take Baptism, for example. If today so many priests, not to speak
of laity, see no need whatsoever for the baptismal blessing of water

and are perfectly satisfied with pouring some holy water into the baptismal font, it is because they do not experience this blessing as the sacramental re-creation of the cosmos so that it may become that which it was intended to be, a gift of God to man, a means of man's knowledge of God and communion with Him. Yet when deprived of this cosmic connotation, the understanding of Baptism itself begins to be altered, and this is exactly what we see in post-patristic theology as well as in post-patristic piety. From regeneration and re-creation, new birth and new life, attention shifts to original sin and justification, and thus to an altogether different theological and spiritual content. If one has all but forgotten the initial and organic connection of Baptism with Pascha and Eucharist; if Baptism ceased to be a paschal sacrament and Pascha a baptismal celebration, it is because one does not experience Baptism as a fundamental act of *passage* from "this world" into the Kingdom of God — an act which, making us die here "in the likeness of Christ's Death," makes our life to be hidden with Christ in God. But again, deprived of this eschatological connotation, Baptism is less and less connected — in theology and piety — with Christ's Death and Resurrection, and indeed post-patristic manuals hardly even mention that connection, as well as the connection of Chrismation with the Pentecostal inauguration of the "new *aeon*."

Take the Eucharist as another example. If it has become one "means of grace" among many; if its aim has been reduced, in theology and piety, to individual edification and sanctification at the virtually total exclusion of any other aspect; it is because its ecclesiological, and this means cosmic and eschatological, dimensions have been simply ignored within the new and "westernized" theological perspective. It is almost amazing how the sacramental theology which developed within that perspective neglected, to say the least, such essential aspects of the Eucharistic *ordo* as the Synaxis, the proclamation of the Gospel, the Offering, the Eucharist itself; and, more importantly, the interdependence of all these aspects and their organic connection with consecration and communion, as well as the specific relationship of Eucharist to time manifested in the uniquely Christian institution of the Lord's Day. All this is simply absent from theology; but then, at the same time, the Eucharist ceases to be experienced as the sacrament of the Church, of her very nature as *passage* and ascension into the Kingdom of God. Theology exhausts itself in purely formal and truly irrelevant definitions of sacrifice and transubstantiation, while piety little by little subordinates the Eucharist to its individualistic and pietistic demands.

To that kind of theology and that kind of piety, meaningless indeed would appear the affirmation that the Eucharist and indeed all sacraments and the entire *leitourgia* of the Church always place us at the beginning and at the end of all things, revealing thus their true meaning and destiny in Christ; that it is the very function or *leitourgia* of the Church's cult — in its structure and rhythm, in its ineffable and celestial beauty, in its words as well as its rites — to be the true epiphany of new creation redeemed by Christ, the presence and power in "this world" of the joy and peace in the Holy Spirit, of the new *aeon* of the Kingdom; and being all this, to be the source and the focus *par excellence* of the Church's faith and theology.

All this is neither "heard" nor understood today, be it by theology or liturgical piety. The former is imprisoned in its own "data" and "propositions," and having eyes does not see and having ears does not hear. The latter is entangled in all kinds of liturgical experiences save the one expressed in the *lex ordandi* itself. And if today the Christian community is being alienated more and more from both; if in theology it sees nothing but intellectual speculations interesting to professionals alone; if liturgy is for it, at best, "inspiration" and, at worst, a meaningless "obligation" to be reduced, if possible, to a valid minimum; the reason for all this is the mutual alienation from one another of theology and liturgy, their surrender to western categories and dichotomies. My last question is: can this alienation be overcome?

VI

Enough has been said above, I think, to enable us to give this question a positive answer: Yes, it can. But only if the theological mind recovers its "wholeness" broken by centuries of western captivity; if it returns to the old yet always valid expression of that wholeness: *lex orandi est lex credendi*. And this implies, as its first condition, a double task: a liturgical critique of theology and a theological critique of the liturgy. In this paper I can only briefly outline my understanding of this double task.

To affirm that liturgy is the source *par excellence* of theology does not mean, as some seem to think, a reduction of theology to liturgy, its transformation into "liturgical theology." The latter appeared (as I tried to explain elsewhere[2]) only as a result of the unhealthy mutual alienation between theology and liturgy, and is therefore a kind of illegitimate child of an illegitimate situation. All theology, indeed, ought to be "liturgical," yet not in the sense of having liturgy as its unique "object" of study, but in that of having its ultimate term of reference in the faith of the Church as manifested and communicated in the liturgy; that catholic vision and experience which it now lacks in its alienation from liturgy.

The western influence upon our theology expressed itself, first of all, in the organization of theological work. Theology, in fact, was broken into a multiplicity of virtually "autonomous" disciplines each depending on its own set of "data" and on its own method, without any clear principle of coordination and theological "integration" into a common vision; indeed, without any common goal. While in the Roman Church such a principle lies

2. In "Liturgical Theology, Theology of Liturgy, and Liturgical Reform," pp. 39–40 and 46–47 above.

in the hierarchical *magisterium,* understood as an authority extrinsic to theology itself; while Protestants do not even claim to have, beyond sufficiently vague "confessions," any consistent theology as theology of the Church; Orthodox theology found itself in a peculiar and unhealthy situation. It adopted, on the one hand and quite uncritically, the western "scientific" organization of theological work, which meant in fact its progressive atomization into a number of uncoordinated and independent "disciplines"; yet, on the other hand, it failed to seek and to determine the criteria and methods that would integrate these disciplines not only into a consistent whole but an adequate and living expression of the Church's faith itself. While adopting methods hitherto alien to it, Orthodox theology did not ask the preliminary question: how are they to express the *experience* of the Church? We have thus dogmatic theology built more or less after the pattern of scholastic theology with its dependence upon "data" and "propositions"; scriptural theology split between a surrender to and a violent rejection of western "criticism," a split leading either to a mere rejection of western critical theories or an equally western fundamentalism; and, finally, a host of "historical" and "practical" disciplines whose relationship to theology as such remains chronically ambiguous and problematic. Not only is there virtually no communication between these disciplines, but their very structure and self-definition prevents each one of them and all of them together from being the *catholic,* i.e., whole and adequate, expression of the Church's faith and experience.

If, however, as I tried to indicate above, it is the very function of the *leitourgia* to be the "epiphany" of the Church's faith, to "make the Church what she is," then theology must find its way back to that source, and rediscover in it precisely that common ground, that initial wholeness and vision which it so obviously lacks now in its topical and methodological fragmentation. If a certain degree of specialization is obviously necessary because it is beneficial to theology's scientific progress, this specialization not only does not exclude, but indeed requires as a very condition of its success and as its inner justification the convergence and interdependence of all disciplines as to their common source and their common goal. This common source is the experience of the Church; this common goal is its adequate, consistent and "credible" presentation, explication and, if necessary, defense. If theology stems from the Church and her experience, it must also lead to the Church and into that experience. In this sense, it is never autonomous, never self-contained and self-sufficient. Its credibility lies not in its rational consistency, but in the fact that it points beyond itself — beyond all words and categories, beyond all formulations and definitions — to that experience and reality which alone gave birth to these words and can alone "authenticate" them.

What then does all this mean in practical terms? In reference to the *leitourgia* as a common source of all theological disciplines it means that whatever a given object of theological scrutiny and investigation, the first and most important "*datum*" is its liturgical experience, its place and connotations within the liturgy. To take but one example, the liturgy of the Paschal *Triduum* — Holy Friday, Great and Holy Saturday and Sunday — reveals more about the "doctrines" of Creation, Fall, Redemption, Death and Resurrection than all other *loci theologici* together; and, let me stress it, not merely in the texts, in the magnificent Byzantine hymnography, but precisely by the very "experience" — ineffable yet illuminating — given during these days in their inner interdependence, in their nature; indeed as epiphany and revelation. Truly if the word *mystery* can still have any meaning today, be experienced and not merely "explained," it is here, in this unique celebration which reveals and communicates before it "explains"; which makes us witnesses and participants of one all-embracing Event from which stems everything else: understanding and power, knowledge and joy, contemplation and communion. It is this experience which then illuminates the theological work proper, be it the exegesis of scripture or patristic texts, or the elaboration in *theoprepeis logoi*, in words adequate to God, of the sacred doctrine, and of its application to the life and the problems of man. It is in the Eucharist, in its *ordo* and movement, in its connection with all other sacraments and cycles of worship, that one discovers the only true and catholic source of ecclesiology in its cosmic as well as eschatological, institutional as well as sacramental, dimensions. It is finally in the "liturgy of time," in the cycles aimed at the sanctification of life, that one first *experiences* the true content of the Christian doctrine of the world and the true meaning of Christian eschatology, before one begins to explain and to elaborate them.

It is obviously impossible for us to give here anything but the most superficial analysis of this initial and organic connection between theology and the liturgical experience of the Church as the primary spring and "ignition" of theology. The liturgical critique of theology is precisely to supply us with such analysis: to rediscover the once living and efficient interdependence of these two essential *leitourgias* of the Church.

As to the liturgy as the common goal of the various theological disciplines, the affirmation *lex orandi est lex credendi* means that it is again in the mystery of the Church that theology finds its inner fulfillment both as theological synthesis and as experience which (although it is itself beyond theology proper, beyond its words and formulations) not only makes them "credible" but indeed *essential* and *authentic.* Theology is always an invitation "to taste and see," an announcement and a promise to be fulfilled in communion, vision and life. The biblical exegesis, the historical analysis, the doctrinal elaboration ultimately converge in and prepare the celebration: the act of witnessing to and participating in the *mystery* itself; that epiphany of life, light and knowledge without which all words remain inescapably "human" — all too human.

All this, however, requires not only a "conversion" of theology itself, of its structure and methods, but, first of all, of the *theologian*. He has mastered to perfection the necessary asceticism of intellectual discipline and integrity, the humility proper to all genuine rational effort. He now has to learn how to immerse himself in the joy of the Church, that great joy with which the disciples returned to Jerusalem to be "continually in the temple blessing God" (Lk 23:52-53). He has to rediscover the oldest of all languages of the Church: that of her rites, the rhythm and the *ordo* of her *leitourgia* in which she concealed from the eyes of "this world" her most precious treasure: the knowledge of that which "no eye has seen, nor ear heard, nor the heart of man conceived, what God has prepared for those who love Him" (1 Cor 2:9). He has to become again not only the student of the Church's faith but, above all, its *witness*.

More than that, if theology needs a "liturgical critique," liturgy — to be again the *leitourgia* of the Church in the full meaning of that term — needs a "theological critique." During the long centuries of its divorce from theology, this meaning, as was said already, has been obscured by several strata of pseudo-theological and pseudo-pious explanations and interpretations, by a superficial pseudo-symbolism, by individualism and legalism. And it is not easy today — when so much of all this has been identified by so many with the very essence of Orthodoxy; has almost become the touchstone of "true" piety and "conservatism" — to rediscover and to communicate the real "key" of the Orthodox liturgical tradition, to connect it again to the *lex credendi*.

Here the task of theology is needed. Here its tradition of intellectual integrity, historical criticism and *acribeia* can make its greater contribution. To do so, however, theology must turn its attention to the *lex orandi*, consider it not only as a source but also as an *object* of its research and study. It is indeed a paradox that the universally admired liturgical tradition of the Eastern Church has

been virtually ignored in both its history and its theological
"content." Not only has theology been divorced from liturgy as
"source," but it paid very little attention to it even as to one of its
"objects." We still have not so much as a complete and critical
history of Byzantine worship in all its aspects. Even here the only
interest shown so far was mainly that by western scholars. Even
here, in their own past and tradition, Orthodox liturgiologists
have remained hopelessly determined in their approach, in their
"problematics," by western scholarship. Yet it is precisely the task
of Orthodox theologians to aim their study of our liturgical
tradition at its overall significance within the Tradition of the
Church, to give it ultimately its true place within the Orthodox
theological enterprise.

To achieve this, however, the study of the liturgy must, on the
one hand, break through the typically western "fixation" on certain themes and problems to the exclusion of many others; and,
on the other hand, overcome the dead ends of self-sufficient
"historicism." It so happened, for example, that under the influence of western theological options, the approach to the Eucharist
was reduced to two or three aspects: those of sacrifice, validity,
and communion, while all that which constitutes the only possible context even for the proper formulation of these aspects, i.e.,
the liturgical *ordo* of the Eucharistic celebration, the interdependence within it of the Synaxis, the liturgy of the Word, the Offertory, the Eucharist, etc., has been virtually ignored. But perhaps
the most important omission was that of the essentially *eschatological* nature of the *leitourgia* — its ultimate relation to and dependence upon the central object of Christian faith, i.e., the
Kingdom of God; that its antinomical relation to time, a relation
constituting virtually the very content of the *Typikon* and all is
"rubrics," that its expression in *beauty:* singing, hymnography,
iconography, ritual, solemnity, that its organic link with matter
are not "accidental," but indeed *essential*; that the epiphany of
"heaven on earth," the icon and fragrance, the beauty and the

ruah of the Kingdom of God, was concealed, so to speak, from theology; reduced, as it were, to the legalistic and rational categories of the western approach to liturgy.

The same can be said of the *historical* reduction of more recent liturgiology, its fixation on the historical development of rites and services, but without any ultimate theological interest and attention. Absolutely indispensable as it is, this historical aspect not only can never be an end in itself, but, in the last analysis, it is only from a theological perspective that it can receive its most important and proper questions. Very good and knowledgeable historians, because of their theological ignorance, have nevertheless produced monuments of nonsense comparable to those produced by the theologians of liturgy ignorant of its history.

At this point, therefore, it is the liturgiologist who must again become a theologian, adopt a theological context and depth for his work. It is indeed the entire Church — clergy and faithful alike — who, in spite of all "pseudomorphoses" still continue to live by the liturgy and from it, must in *lex orandi* rediscover the *lex credendi*, and make their liturgical piety a way of theological knowledge and understanding.

Ultimately, the liturgical problem of our time is thus a problem of restoring to liturgy its theological meaning, and to theology its liturgical dimension. Just as theology cannot recover its central place and function within the Church without being rooted again in the very experience of the Church, liturgy cannot be rescued from its present decay by hasty, superficial and purely external reforms aimed at meeting vague and doubtful "needs" of a mythological "modern man." For what this "modern man," his culture, and his society ultimately seek is not a Church that would serve them by adopting their "image," but the Church that would fulfill the Divine mission by being always and everywhere the *epiphany:* the gift and communication of the eternal Mystery of Salvation; and by being this, would reveal to man his true nature and destiny. Theology must rediscover as its own "rule of faith" the Church's *lex orandi*, and the liturgy reveal itself again as the *lex credendi*.

5

Theology and Eucharist

I

The actual state of Orthodox theology must be characterized by two words: confusion and awakening.[1] By confusion, I mean an obvious lack of unity among Orthodox theologians: unity of theological language, unity of method, consensus as to the nature of questions and the mode of their solution. Our theology develops in a plurality of theological "keys" and within several mutually exclusive intellectual frameworks. This confusion, however, is also the sign of an awakening, of a new search for a genuinely Orthodox theological perspective.

This situation is by no means accidental, for the fate of Orthodox theology has been a tragic one. On the one hand, since the collapse of Byzantium and the interruption of the creative patristic tradition, our theology endured a long "western captivity" which deeply obscured and even deformed the Orthodox theological mind, while, on the other hand, the same post-patristic period was that of a radical transformation of the status and function of theology in the life of the Church. From being the concern — and the function — of the whole Church, it became that of the "school" alone and was thus deprived of the living interest and attention without which no creative effort is possible. Today the situation is changing. Conflicts and divisions within the Church, the new "ecumenical" encounter with the Christian West, and, above all, the pressing challenge of the modern world, have placed theology in a new focus, restored to it an importance it has not

1. Originally appeared in *St Vladimir's Seminary Quarterly*, 5, 1961, pp. 10-23.

had for many centuries. Hence both the confusion and the awakening, the unavoidable clash between ideas, the pluralism of approaches, the acuteness of the methodological problem, the new questioning of sources and authorities. Freed from official "conformity" which was imposed on it by extra-theological factors, Orthodox theology has not yet found a real unity. But it must find it. However understandable and even useful, the actual theological pluralism cannot last forever. It is a *synthesis*, i.e., an integration of all the more or less "private" theologies into one consistent whole, that we must seek. For Orthodox theology is by its very nature a catholic expression of the Church's faith and the Church neither knows nor needs any other theology.

II

But *synthesis* here means something different from a purely formal agreement on the sources to be cited or the formulas to be used as safely Orthodox. As long as there exist theologians (and not only compilers and commentators of ancient texts) theology will remain a symphony, not a unison. What is meant here is an inner transformation of the theological mind itself, a transformation based on a new — or maybe on a very old — relationship between theology and the Church. It is indeed our first duty to acknowledge that for centuries theology was *alienated* from the Church and that this alienation had tragic consequences for both theology and the Church. It made theology a merely intellectual activity, split into scores of "disciplines" with no correlation among themselves and no application to the real needs of the Church. Theology ceased to be the answer the Church gives to her questions and, having ceased to be such an answer, it also ceased to be the question addressed to the Church. It today constitutes within the Church a self-centered world, virtually isolated from the Church's life. It lives in itself and by itself in tranquil academic quarters, well defended against profane intrusions and curiosities by a highly technical language. Theologians avoid discussing the trivial reality of the Church's life, and do not even dream about influencing it in any way. In turn, the Church, i.e., the bishops, priests and laity, are supremely indifferent to the writings of the theologians, even when they do not regard them with open suspicion. No wonder, therefore, that deprived of interest on the part of the Church, squeezed into the narrow limits of a professional clerical school, theology is guided in its inner life not by the experience, needs or problems of the Church but by individual interests of individual theologians. Liberal or conservative, neo-patristic or neo-mystical, historical or anti-historical, "ecumenical" or anti-western (and we have at present all these brands), theology simply fails to reach anybody but professionals, to provoke anything but esoteric controversies in academic periodicals.

And yet this isolation and alienation of theology is a tragedy for the Church as well. For although the ecclesiastical leaders and the people may not realize it, and think (as they too often do) that all problems and difficulties can be solved by better administration and simple references to the past, the Church *needs* theology. Its vital and essential function is to constantly refer the empirical life of the Church to the very sources of her faith and life, to the living and life-giving Truth, and to evaluate and judge the "empirical" in the light of that Truth. Ideally theology is the conscience of the Church, her purifying self-criticism, her permanent reference to the ultimate goals of her existence. Deprived of theology, of its testimony and judgment, the Church is always in danger of forgetting and misinterpreting her own Tradition, confusing the essential with the secondary, absolutizing the contingent, losing the perspective of her life. She becomes a prisoner of her "empirical" needs and the pragmatic spirit of "this world" which poisons and obscures the absolute demands of the Truth.

If theology, then, needs the Church as its natural "term of reference," as both the source and the aim of its very existence, and if the Church needs theology as her conscience, how can they be reunited again, overcome their mutual alienation and recover the organic correlation of which the Patristic age remains forever the ideal pattern? This is the question Orthodox theology must answer if it is to overcome its inner chaos and weakness, its parasitic existence in the Church which pays no attention to it.

How and where? My answer is — by and in the Eucharist, understood and lived as the Sacrament of the Church, as the act which ever makes the Church to be what she is — the People of God, the Temple of the Holy Spirit, the Body of Christ, the gift and manifestation of the new life of the new age. It is here and only here, in the unique center of all Christian life and experience that theology can find again its fountain of youth, be regenerated as a living testimony to the living Church, her faith, love and hope. This affirmation, I understand it only too well, can be easily misunderstood. It will appear to some as an unjustified reduction of theology to "liturgics," as an unnecessary narrowing of the proper field of theology, where the Eucharist is listed as just one of the sacraments, as an "object" among many. To others it will sound like a pious invitation to theologians to become more liturgical, more "eucharistic" . . . . In the present state of theology, such misinterpretations would be almost natural. What is meant here, however, is not a reduction of theology to piety, be it theological piety or a piety of theologians, and although it will take more than a short article to elaborate the answer given above in all its implications, the following remarks may possibly prepare the ground for a more constructive discussion.

III

In the official, post-patristic and "westernizing" theology, the Eucharist is treated merely as one of the sacraments. Its place in ecclesiology is that of a "means of grace" — one among many. However central and essential in the life of the Church, the

Eucharist is *institutionally* distinct from the Church. It is the power, the grace given to the Church that makes the Eucharist possible, valid, efficient, but this power of grace "precedes" the Eucharist and is virtually independent from it. Thus the Church is understood and described here as an institution endowed with divine power: power to teach, to guide, to sanctify; as a structure for the communication of grace; a "power," however, which is not derived from the Eucharist. The latter is a fruit, a result of the Church, not her source. And, likewise, being the cause of her sacraments, the Church is not considered in any way as their aim or goal. For official theology it is always the satisfaction of the individual, not the fulfillment or edification of the Church, that constitutes the end and the purpose of a sacrament.

This type of theology, although it subordinates the Eucharist and the sacraments to the Church and makes the latter an institution distinct and independent from the sacraments, easily coexists with, if indeed it is not responsible for, a piety in which the Church is virtually identified with cult or worship. In the popular approach — and "popular" by no means excludes the great majority of the clergy — the Church is, above all, a "cultic" or liturgical institution, and all her activities are, implicitly or explicitly, directed at her liturgical needs: erection of temples, material support of clergy and choirs, acquisition of various liturgical supplies, etc. Even the teaching given to the faithful, if one abstracts from it a very vague and general ethical code, identical with the humanistic ethics of the secular society at large, consists mainly in liturgical prescriptions and obligations of all kinds. The institutional priority of the Church over her sacrament is not questioned here, but the Church is essentially an institution existing for the fulfillment of the "religious needs" of her members, and since worship in all its forms constitutes the most obvious and immediate of such needs, the understanding and experience of the Church as existing primarily *for* liturgy seems quite natural.

While "institution" for theology and "worship" for piety, the
Church is nowhere a "society." And indeed, although the classical
catechetical definition of the Church as society has never been
openly revised or rejected, the Church-society simply does not
manifest herself outside the common attendance of worship. Yet
the experience of worship has long ago ceased to be that of a
corporate liturgical act. It is an aggregation of individuals coming
to church, attending worship in order to satisfy individually their
individual religious needs, not in order to *constitute* and to *fulfill*
the Church. The best proof of this is the complete disintegration
of communion as a corporate act. Where the early Church saw
her real fulfillment as a communion into one body ("... and unite
all of us who partake of the one Bread and the one Cup, one to
another ..." [Liturgy of St Basil]), we today consider Communion
as the most individual and private of all religious acts, depending
entirely on one's personal desire, piety and preparation. Likewise
the sermon, although addressed to the congregation, is, in fact, a
personal teaching, aimed not at the "edification" of the Church,
but at individuals — at their private needs and duties. Its theme is
the individual Christian, not the Church.

IV

It is true, on the theological level at least, that the theology and
the piety described above, are criticized, denounced as obviously
one-sided and deficient. If nothing else, the social and socially
oriented "ethos" of our time was bound to provoke a reaction
against an ecclesiology in which institutional absolutism is com-
bined with spiritual individualism, the "objectivity" of the
Church with an amazingly "subjective" religious life. Hence a
new interest in the status and nature of the laity, in the corporate
aspects of worship, a new search for a more complete definition of
the Church, the scrutinizing of the scriptural concepts of Body,
People, etc.; hence also the emphasis on "participation" in the

liturgical movement.

The reaction is, no doubt, a good and promising one. Yet, one extreme can easily lead to another and this is the danger we face today. Paradoxically enough the danger arises from the very source of our ecclesiological revival — the rediscovery of the "social" and the "organic" as essential dimensions of the Church. If, in the past, the Church was identified too exclusively with hierarchy and institution, there is a tendency now to just as exclusively identify her with an "organism." The Fathers, we are told, have not left with us any precise definition of the Church's *nature* or *essence*. Consequently, theologians reconstruct what seems to them to be the patristic ecclesiology, not discerning too often that, in fact, this overwhelmingly "organic" ecclesiology reflects some contemporary philosophical and sociological doctrines more than the experience of the early Church. The Church is a society, this society is an organism, this organism is the Body of Christ. Such a sequence of direct identifications, typical of the present ecclesiological trend, gives the idea of "organism" an almost biological connotation. It makes the Church a *substantial Being*, whose "organic unity" and "organic life" overshadow the personal, spiritual and dynamic aspects of unity and life. Unity is no longer understood as, first of all, the union of many, fulfilling itself in unity, *becoming* unity; it is a reality in which one "participates" and the category of participation leaves almost no room for that of becoming and fulfillment. The Church is a given reality, an organism whose life is conveyed and communicated to its members through the sacraments, the latter, and especially the Eucharist, being the means of this communication and participation.

It is very doubtful, however, whether to begin the definition of the Church in terms of "organism" is a good ecclesiological beginning at all. The absence of such a definition in the Fathers may not have been accidental, but rather a revealing experience of

the Church which we have not yet fully grasped. In the patristic
perspective, the Church is primarily the gift of new life, but this
life is not that *of the Church*, but the life of Christ in us, our life in
Him. For the Church is not a "being" in the sense in which God
or man may be called "beings" ("hypostasized natures," to use the
ancient terminology), she is not a new "nature" added to the
existing natures of God and man, she is not a "substance." The
term *new* applied to her — new life, new creation — does not
mean an ontological newness, the appearance of a "being" which
did not exist before; it means the redeemed, renewed and transfigured relationship between the only "substantial" beings: God and
His creation. And just as the Church has no "hypostasis" or
"personality" of her own, other than the hypostasis of Christ and
those of the people who constitute her, she has no "nature" of her
own, for she is the new life of the "old" nature, redeemed and
transfigured by Christ. In Him man, and through man the whole
of "nature," find their true life and become a new creation, a new
being, the Body of Christ. Thus, on the one hand, there exists in
the iconographic tradition of Orthodoxy no icon of the Church,
because an icon implies necessarily a "hypostasized nature," the
reality of a substantial and personal "being," and in this sense the
Church is not a "being." Yet, on the other hand, each icon — that
of Christ, of the Theotokos, of any saint — is always and essentially an icon of the Church, because it manifests and reveals the
new life of a being, the reality of its transfiguration, of its passage
into the "new *aeon*" of the Holy Spirit, this being precisely the
manifestation of the Church. Therefore, the concepts of "organism" or "body" can be utterly misleading if, in a definition of the
Church, they precede and give foundation to, that of "life." It is
not because she is an "organism" that the Church gives us the
"new life," but the new life given in her, or rather, the Church as
a new life, *makes* us an organism, transforms us into the Body of
Christ, reveals us as "new being."

  We see now that the ecclesiological equation "institution —

society — organism — Body of Christ" needs to be qualified. It would be a great error directly to apply the scriptural and traditional term "Body of Christ" to the Church as institution or society. In itself, "institution," "society" — i.e., the visible, militant, hierarchical Church — is not the new life, the new being and the new age. It belongs to the structure and reality of the history of salvation and, therefore, to "this world." But just as the Church of the Old Covenant, the old Israel, existed as a *passage* to the New Covenant, was *instituted* in order to prepare the ways of the Lord, the Church as *institution* exists in order to reveal — in "this world" — the "world to come," the Kingdom of God, fulfilled and manifested in Christ. She is the *passage* of the "old" into the "new" — yet what is being redeemed, renewed and transfigured through her is not the "Church," but the old life itself, the old Adam and the whole of creation. And she is this "passage" precisely because as institution she is "bone of the bones and flesh of the flesh" of this world, because she stands for the whole creation, truly represents it, assumes all of its life and offers it — in Christ — to God. She is indeed *instituted* for the world and not as a separate "religious" institution existing for the specifically religious needs of men. She represents — "makes present" — the whole of mankind, because mankind and creation were called from the very beginning to be the Temple of the Holy Spirit and the receptacle of Divine life. The Church is thus the restoration by God and the acceptance by humanity of the original and eternal destiny of creation itself. She is the presence of the Divine Act which restores and the obedience of people who accept this act. Yet it is only when she performs and fulfills this "passage," when, in other terms, she transcends herself as "institution" and "society" and becomes indeed the new life of the new creation, that she *is* the Body of Christ. As institution the Church is in *this world* the sacrament of the Body of Christ, of the Kingdom of God and the world to come.

We recover thus the *eschatological* dimension of the Church.

The body of Christ is not and can never be *of* this world. "This world" condemned Christ, the bearer of new life, to death and by doing this it has condemned itself to death. The new life which shone forth from the grave is the life of the "new *aeon*," of the age which in terms of this world is still "to come." The descent of the Holy Spirit at Pentecost, by inaugurating a new *aeon*, announced the *end* of this world, for as no one can partake of the "new life" without dying in the baptismal death, no one can have Christ as his *life* unless he has died and is constantly dying to this world: "For you have died, and your life is hid with Christ in God" (Col 3:3). But then nothing which is of this world — no institution, no society, no church — can be identified with the new *aeon*, the new being. The most perfect Christian community — be it completely separated from the evils of the world — as a community is still *of* this world, living its life, depending on it. It is only by *passing* into the new *aeon*, by an anticipation — in faith, hope and love — of the world to come, that a community can partake of the Body of Christ, and indeed manifest itself as the Body of Christ. The Body of Christ can never be "part" of this world, for Christ has ascended into heaven and his Kingdom is Heaven...

V

We can now return to the Eucharist, for it is indeed the very *act of passage* in which the Church fulfills herself as a new creation and, therefore, *the* Sacrament of the Church. In the Eucharist, the Church transcends the dimensions of "institution" and becomes the Body of Christ. It is the *"Eschaton"* of the Church, her manifestation as the world to come.

We have said that if, on the one hand, our "westernizing" theology subordinates the Eucharist (as "effect") to the Church (as "cause"), the common Orthodox piety, on the other hand, experiences the Church as a "liturgical institution," as cult. But if there is any truth in the preceding discussion of ecclesiology, the relationship Church-Liturgy, or more exactly, Church-Eucharist, must be reversed. It is not the Church that exists for, or "generates," the liturgy; it is the Eucharist which, in a very real sense, "generates" the Church, makes her to be what she is. We know that originally the Greek word *leitourgia* had no cultic connotations. It meant a public office, a service performed on behalf of a community and for its benefit. In the Septuagint, the word naturally acquired a religious meaning, yet still not necessarily a "liturgical" one. It implied the same idea of service, applied now to the chosen people of God whose specific *leitourgia* is to fulfill God's design in history, to prepare the "way of the Lord." The early Christian use reflected the same meaning of *leitourgia.* The fact that the church adopted it finally for her cult, and especially for the Eucharist, indicates her special understanding of worship which is indeed a revolutionary one. If Christian worship is *leitourgia,* it cannot be simply reduced to, or expressed in terms of, "cult." The ancient world knew a plethora of cultic religions or "cults" — in which worship or cultic acts were the only real content of religion, an "end in itself." But the Christian cult is *leitourgia,* and this means that it is *functional* in its essence, has a goal to achieve which transcends the categories of cult as such. This goal is precisely the *Church* as the manifestation and presence of the "new *aeon,*" of the Kingdom of God. In a sense the Church is indeed a *liturgical institution,* i.e. an institution whose *leitourgia* is to fulfill itself as the Body of Christ and a new creation. Christian cult is, therefore, a radically new cult, unprecedented in both the Old Testament and paganism, and the deficiency of a certain theology, as well as of a certain liturgical piety, is that they not only overlook the radical newness of Christian *leitourgia,* but rather define and experience it again in the old cultic categories.

Such is the distortion, however, of our present ecclesiology that to affirm the uniqueness of the Eucharist as *the sacrament of the Church,* raises at once the question of its relation to the other sacraments, which in official theology are considered as separate "means of grace," practically independent from one another. Nothing reveals more the neglect of the living Tradition than the post-patristic sacramental theology. It begins with a general theology of sacraments, which is then "applied" to each particular sacrament. As to Tradition, it follows exactly the opposite order. It begins with specific liturgical acts which not only are organically related to one another, but necessarily *refer* to the Eucharist as to their fulfillment, as, indeed, to the "sacrament of sacraments." That ordination, for example, is to be performed within the Eucharist, that each of our three orders are, in ordination, related to a particular moment of the Eucharistic liturgy, is for the dogmatician a secondary liturgical detail with no real impact on the "essence" of the sacrament. In the living tradition, however, this relation is of paramount importance and reveals more about the "nature of the ministry" than any of the countless scholastic treatises written on the subject. There exists between the Eucharist and each of the other sacraments an organic link. For all the sacraments, except the Eucharist, deal with individual members of the Church and their purpose is to *integrate* the individual — his life, his particular *leitourgia* or calling — into the Church. But the Church is fulfilled in the Eucharist, and each sacrament, therefore, finds its natural *end*, its fulfillment in the Eucharist.

The theology of manuals stresses the sacramental power of the Church or, in other words, the Church as the "distributor of grace." But it overlooks almost completely the Church as the end and fulfillment of the sacraments. For grace is another name for the Church in the state of fulfillment as the manifestation of the age of the Holy Spirit. There has occurred a very significant shift in the understanding of the sacraments. They have become private services for individual Christians, aimed at their personal sanctification, not at the edification of the Church. The sacrament of penance, for example, which was originally an act of reconciliation *with* the Church is understood today as mere "power of absolution." Matrimony, which at first even had no special "liturgy" of its own and was performed through the participation of a newly-wed couple in the Eucharist, is no longer considered as the *passage* — and, therefore, transformation — of a "natural" marriage into the dimensions of the Church, "... for this is a great mystery, *but* I speak concerning Christ and the Church" (Eph 5:32), but is defined as a "blessing" bestowed upon husband and wife, as a simple Christian sanction of marriage. The Eucharistic cup is replaced in it by a cup "symbolizing" common life. Examples like these can be multiplied. But no theological deformation and no piety, based on this deformation, can ultimately obscure and alter the fundamental and organic connection of all sacraments with the Eucharist, as the sacrament of sacraments, and, therefore, truly *the* Sacrament of the Church.

VI

Having forgotten the ecclesiological and the eschatological significance of the Eucharist, having reduced it to one "means of grace" among many, our official theology was bound to limit the theological study of the Eucharist to only two problems: that of the transformation of the bread and wine into the Body and Blood of Christ and that of communion. As applied to the Eucharist, the term "sacrament" usually means either one of these acts or both, although it is explicitly admitted that they can be treated separately. Within this theological framework the Church remains mainly as a "power" — to perform the transformation, to give communion. The priest is the minister (the "performer") of the sacrament; the elements of bread and wine — its "matter"; the communicant — its recipient. But communion having long ago ceased to be a self-evident fulfillment of the sacrament — 90% of our eucharistic celebrations are without communicants — there developed an additional and virtually independent theology of the Eucharist as sacrifice, essential *per se*, regardless of the people's presence or participation. And finally, since theology by focusing its attention on these two moments of the Eucharist imperceptibly relegated all other elements of the eucharistic celebration into the category of "non-essential" rituals, the door was open to their interpretation in terms of *liturgical symbolism.* As understood and explained since Cabasilas, the Eucharist is a symbolical representation of the life of Christ, serving as a framework for the double sacrament of consecration and communion, yet not essential for its "validity" and "efficacy."

But from the standpoint of Tradition the sacramental character of the Eucharist cannot be artificially narrowed to one act, to one moment of the whole rite. We have an "*ordo*" in which all parts and all elements are essential, are organically linked together in one sacramental structure. In other words, the Eucharist is a sacrament from the beginning to the end and its fulfillment or consummation is "made possible" by the entire liturgy. Liturgy here is not opposed to sacrament, as "symbolism" to "realism," but indeed *is* sacrament: one, organic, consistent passage, in which each step prepares and "makes possible" the following one.

For the Eucharist, we have said, is a *passage,* a procession leading the Church into "heaven," into her fulfillment as the Kingdom of God. And it is precisely the reality of this passage into the *Eschaton* that conditions the transformation of our offering — bread and wine — into the new food of the new creation, of our meal into the Messianic Banquet and the *Koinonia* of the Holy Spirit. Thus, for example, the coming together of Christians on the Lord's Day, their visible unity "sealed" by the priest (*ecclesia in episcopo* and *episcopus in ecclesia*) is indeed the beginning of the sacrament, the "gathering *into* the Church." And the *entrance* is not a symbolical representation of Christ going to preach but the *real* entrance — the beginning of the Church's ascension to the Throne of God, made possible, inaugurated by the ascension of Christ's Humanity. The offertory — the solemn transfer of bread and wine to the altar is again not the symbol of Christ's burial (or of His entrance into Jerusalem) but a real sacrifice — the *transfer* of our lives and bodies and of the whole "matter" of the whole creation into heaven, their integration in the unique and all-embracing sacrifice of all sacrifices, that of Christ. The *prosphora* (offering) makes possible the *anaphora* — the lifting up of the Church, her eschatological fulfillment by the *Eucharist.* For Eucharist — "thanksgiving" — is indeed the very content of the redeemed life, the very *reality* of the Kingdom as "joy and peace in the Holy Spirit," the end and the fulfillment of our ascension into heaven. Therefore, the Eucharist *is* consecration and the Fathers called both the prayer of consecration and the consecrated gifts "Eucharist." The insistence by the Orthodox on the *epiclesis* is nothing else, in its ultimate meaning, but the affirmation that the consecration, i.e., the transformation of bread and wine into the Body and Blood of Christ, takes place in the "new *aeon*" of the Holy Spirit. Our earthly food *becomes* the Body and Blood of Christ because it has been assumed, accepted, lifted up into the "age to come," where Christ is indeed the very life, the very food of all life and the Church in His Body, "the fullness of Him that fills all in all" (Eph 1:23). It is there, finally, that we partake of the food of immortality, are made participants of the Messianic Banquet, of the New Pascha; it is from there, "having seen the true light, having received the heavenly Spirit," that we return into "this world" ("let us depart in peace") as witnesses of the Kingdom which is "to come." Such is the sacrament of the Church, the *leitourgia* which eternally transforms the Church into what she is, makes her the Body of Christ and the Temple of the Holy Spirit.

VII

The reader may get the impression that I have forgotten the initial theme of this paper — theology in its relation to the Church. The preceding developments were necessary, however, for it is only after the terms of reference have been defined that we can now try to explain what was meant by the affirmation made above about the Eucharist as the source of theology, as the way of the latter's reintegration into the Church.

In the past years we have been often told that Orthodox theology, if it wants to overcome its inner weakness and deficiencies, must *return to the Fathers.* "Patristic revival," "neo-patristic synthesis" — these and similar expressions are frequent in current Orthodox writings and they point, no doubt, to a very genuine and urgent need. The interruption of the living patristic tradition was indeed the origin of the great theological tragedy of Orthodoxy. But what exactly is meant by this "return" and how are we to perform it? To these questions no satisfactory answer has been given. Does it mean a mere repetition of what the Fathers said, on the assumption that they have said everything that is essential and nothing is needed but a recapitulation of their consensus? Such an assumption, even if it were a valid one, would certainly not solve the problem, as we stated it before — that of the present theological *alienation.* No collection of highly technical patrological monographs, no edition of patristic texts for the common use, would constitute in themselves the living and creative answer to the real questions of our time, or the real needs of the Church. There would still be the necessity of interpreting the patristic message, of its "resurrection" in the mind of the Church, or, in other words, the problem of the theological "breaking through." But we must remember that the Church has never taught that the Fathers answered all questions, that their theology is the whole theology and that the theologian today is merely a commentator of patristic texts. To transform the Fathers into a purely formal and infallible authority, and theology into a patristic scholasticism is, in fact, a betrayal of the very spirit of patristic theology, which remains forever a wonderful example of spiritual freedom and creativity. The "return to the Fathers" means, above all, the recovery of their spirit, of the secret inspiration which made them true witnesses of the Church.

We return indeed to the Fathers, and not only to their "texts," when we recover and make ours the experience of the Church not as mere "institution, doctrine, or system," to quote A S Khomiakov, but as the all-embracing, all-assuming and all-transforming *life*, the passage into the reality of redemption and transfiguration. This experience, as we tried to show, is centered in the Eucharist, the Sacrament of the Church, the very manifestation and self-revelation of the Church. Eucharist, whether it is expressly referred to or not, is the organic source and the necessary "term of reference" of theology, for if theology is bearing witness to the faith and the life of the Church, to the Church as salvation and the new life in Christ, it bears witness primarily to the experience of the Church manifested, communicated and actualized in the Eucharist. It is in the Eucharist that the Church ceases to be "institution, doctrine, system" and becomes Life, Vision, Salvation; it is in the Eucharist that the Word of God is fulfilled and the human mind made capable of expressing the mind of Christ. Here then is the source of theology, of *words about God*, the "event" which transforms our human speculation into a message of Divine Truth.

VIII

I will conclude with two remarks, one dealing with the more immediate theological "agenda" of our time, and the other with the general spirit of Orthodox theology.

1) First of all, there should be no misunderstanding. The "eucharistic conversion" of theology does not mean an imposition on the theologian of a definite program, of a prescribed set of themes and questions. On the contrary, properly understood, it liberates him from the dead authority of pseudo-traditional systems, puts him into direct contact with the whole of *reality*: God, man and the world. "The spirit blows where it wills ..." (Jn 3:8). There exists, however, a preliminary problem, which must be

dealt with, for it constitutes precisely the condition of the "eucharistic conversion" of theology. It is, to put it bluntly, the theological rediscovery of the Eucharist itself. It is here, we have seen, that the official, post-patristic theology has suffered its most obvious, most harmful metamorphosis, has deviated from the living Tradition, has "alienated" itself from the experience of the Church. It is here, therefore, that its deficiencies and limitations must be judged and overcome. To "rediscover" the Eucharist means, as we have tried to show, to recover its ecclesiological and eschatological "fulness," to know it again as the Sacrament of the Church. This, in turn, means that the reduction of the Eucharist to a multiplicity of artificially isolated "questions" — sacrament, sacrifice, communion, etc. — must be transcended in a reintegrated vision and experience. Such reintegration is possible only when one ceases to abstract the Eucharist as "sacrament," "sacrifice" or "communion" from the Eucharistic *leitourgia*, from the action in which all these aspects can be understood in their proper perspective and in their organic relation with one another. The *lex orandi* must be recovered as the *lex credendi*. The rediscovery of the Eucharist as the Sacrament of the Church is, in other words, the rediscovery of the Church *in actu*, the Church as the Sacrament of Christ, of His *"parousia"* — the *coming* and *presence* of the Kingdom which is *to come*.

Let us not be mistaken: the task presents enormous difficulties. So much has been forgotten or neglected. The true meaning of the *leitourgia* of the Church has to be found again. The whole development of the liturgical piety must be reevaluated. The formidable inertia and opposition of dead conservatism and pseudo-traditionalism has to be met and overcome. Theological "regeneration" however, demands this price and nothing short of a *crisis* — constructive criticism, critical reconstruction — can restore theology to its real function within the Church.

2) The term "eucharistic ecclesiology" has been recently intro-

duced into our theological vocabulary. One can speak of even greater reasons for *eucharistic theology*, and this entire essay is nothing but an attempt to prove that truly Orthodox theology is by its very nature "eucharistic." This does not mean that the Eucharist as such is the only object of theological contemplation and analysis. It was precisely such a transformation of the Eucharist into an "object" that obscured its function as the source of theology. It means that in the life of the Church the Eucharist is the *moment of truth* which makes it possible to see the real "objects" of theology: God, man and the world, in the *true light*, which, in other words, reveals both the *objects* of theology as they really are and gives the necessary *light* for their understanding. "We have seen the true light, we have received the Heavenly Spirit..." Theology, like any other Christian service or *leitourgia*, is a *charisma*, a gift of the Holy Spirit. This gift is given *in the Church*, i.e., in the act in which the Church fulfills herself as the communion of the Holy Spirit, in which she offers *in* Christ and offers *Him*, and is accepted *by* Christ and receives *from* Him; in the act which is, therefore, the source of all charisms and ministries of the Church. It is the moment of truth, indeed, for there we stand before God, in Christ who is the End, the *Eschaton*, the Fulness of all our humanity, and in Him offer to God the only "reasonable service" (*logike latreia*) of the redeemed world — the Eucharist, and in the light of it see and understand and recapitulate *in Christ* the truth about God, man and the world, about the creation and fall, sin and redemption, about the whole universe and its final transfiguration in the Kingdom of God, and we receive this truth in participation of the Body and Blood of Christ, in the unending Pentecost that "guides us into all truth and shows us things to come" (Jn 16:13). The task of theology is to bear witness to this truth, and there is no end to this task. Each theologian will see it only partially and partially reflect it, and each one will remain free, indeed, to reflect it according to his own particular charisma and vocation, but just as all charismata have one and the same source, all vocations ultimately contribute to the edification of one catholic theology of the Church.

Return to the Bible, return to the Fathers..., this means, above all, the return to the Church through the Eucharist and to the Eucharist through the Church: here the "texts" of the Scripture are given to us again and again as the living and life-creating Word of God, here we meet our Fathers not in "books" but in reality, the Reality to which they bore witness in their time and in their language, to which we are called to bear witness in our time and in our own language. "For the languages in the world are different," says St Irenaeus, "but the power of tradition is one and the same" (*Adv Haer* 1, 10, 2). "Our teaching," he adds, "is conformed to the Eucharist, and the Eucharist confirms our teaching."

6

Liturgy and Eschatology

The First Nicholas Zernov Memorial Lecture
25 May 1982

It is a great honor and also a joy to be giving this first memorial lecture.[1] Dr Nicholas Zernov, in whose memory this lecture has been established, played a tremendous role in my life and in the life of many of my contemporaries, Russian Orthodox boys growing up in exile — a role of encouragement and inspiration in demanding from us, and showing us an example of, committed and unbroken service to the Orthodox Church. It was so easy for Russians in exile in the 20s and 30s to forget the past and to settle down happily by the waters of Babylon. It is men like Nicholas Zernov who encouraged and inspired us with their own example in maintaining faithfulness to the realities which he himself had served all his life: the Church and Russia, Christian Russia. So it is with real gratitude that I have accepted this invitation. I have been walking round Oxford for two days now and all the time remembering my first meeting with Dr Zernov. I was sixteen years old, and it was at a conference of the Fellowship of St Alban and St Sergius. I didn't speak English, I didn't understand what was discussed. I didn't even attend many of the sessions — I was more interested in playing tennis. But the fact remains that it was there, not in Paris but at that Fellowship conference in Britain, that I discovered the direction which my life was to take. For that I shall always be indebted to Nicholas Zernov.

---

1. First published in *Sobornost*, 7, 1985, pp. 6-14.

A Post-Christian Era?

When I think about contemporary theology and try to understand the meaning of its diversity, of the many trends, ideologies,
confessional emphases that mark it so deeply, I always recall an
expression which for several years now has been popular in some
circles, the expression "post-Christian era." Whatever else that
phrase may signify, it has a certain relevance for anyone seeking a
meaning in contemporary theology. The common assumption of
that theology (in spite of all its confessional and other differences), an assumption made knowingly or unknowingly, is that
theology is being written or thought or believed in a post-Christian era. This is *assumed.* It does not mean that every theologian
writes explicitly about the post-Christian era; on the contrary,
there is much "business as usual" going on in theology. But when
you try to find a unifying principle underlying contemporary
theology, it seems to be this: that we are living, praying and
theologizing in a world from which our Christian faith is divorced; that there is a deep divorce between not just the Church
but the whole Christian world-view on the one hand, and the
culture and society in which we live on the other. This is regarded
as a self-evident assumption. It is not the *theme* of contemporary
theology, but one of its *sources.* It is important for us to try to
understand this experience of divorce.

Theology is and always has been aimed at the world. Theology
is not exclusively for the inner consumption of the Church. There
has always been an effort, on the Christian side, to explain the
Gospel in terms of a given culture, of a given world common-
wealth. And therefore theology has always tried to have a common language with the world in which it is theologizing. The
Fathers of the Church were doing exactly that (not that this
exhausts the meaning of the Patristic era); they were reconciling
Jerusalem and Athens, Athens and Jerusalem, and were coining a
common language which would be faithful to the Gospel while

yet understandable and acceptable to the world. But what is to be done when that common language breaks down, and there is no more common language? For that is our situation today. An era has finished, an era characterized by the existence of the Christian Church, of Christian theology, indeed of a Christian world.

The Radical "Yes": Liberation Theology and Therapeutic Theology

In the face of this divorce, of this breakdown of a common language, two fundamental attitudes in theology tend to develop.

One type of theology — and within it there is a wide-ranging pluralism — still continues to search for a common language with the world, and this it does by adopting what can be described as the discourse proper to the world today. This means, to borrow a phrase that I associate with Fr Congar, that it is the world which sets the agenda for the Church. I vividly remember going about three years ago to a theological bookstore in Paris, where you can find all modern theology in twenty-two minutes. Here I came across the title *A Marxist Reading of St Luke*; a few minutes later I found *A Freudian Reading of St John*. Here, in the titles of these two books and others like them, we see a theology in desperate search for a common language with the world, a theology that finds this common language in the *discours* of the world itself.

This type of theology includes various trends. When concerned more particularly with justice and politics, it may take the form of liberation theology. Another trend within this same type of theology is well described in the title of a book called *The Triumph of Therapeutics*. We develop a therapeutical theology, because our world is therapeutic. We are always trying to help people. I don't know about London, but in New York you cannot miss advertisements for a toothpaste that guarantees happiness. We make the same claim for religion: it also "guarantees happiness." "Take your family to the church or synagogue of your choice. It helps."

Here, then, are two trends, the one concerned with society and the other with the individual. The first derives to some extent from Hegel, with his transformation of history into History with a capital H. The second adopts the view of the individual predominant in the world today, which regards him as a patient in a cosmic hospital, constantly under treatment, yet always with the promise of a total cure and immortality. Here, as in the realm of politics, theology seeks to take a more and more active part: we want to show that we are not behind, that we are catching up with this therapeutic triumph.

The Radical "No": "Spirituality"

But there is also another type of theology, which consists first of all in a rejection of the approach just described. This second type abandons all attempts to achieve a common *discours* between theology and the world. Its main goal (and I am oversimplifying: I can only make the point in outline) is the attainment of personal spiritual self-fulfillment. After being dean of a seminary now for more than twenty years, I notice that the word "spirituality" is pronounced much more often than the name of Jesus Christ. And the spirituality advocated by this second type of theology is above all a spirituality of escape, a highly personal spirituality, without any reference to the world. To use a little paradox: St Anthony the Great, in founding Christian monasticism, was more involved in the emerging Christian world of his time than some of those Christians today who, while living in the world, by all possible means try to escape from it and to ignore its existence.

Such are the two main approaches to theology, each of them containing a great variety of attitudes. Together they constitute what I call the theology of the post-Christian era, because both types, in all their varieties, assume that it is impossible to do anything except think in terms of being "post-Christian." Either we must agree to join the world in its labors, its dreams, perspectives and horizons, or else we must seek a personal, individual escape from the world into a purely "spiritual" realm. Spirituality becomes in this second case a kind of religion in itself, and this helps to explain the many *rapprochements* between Christian and non-Christian spirituality. Even the term "Jesus Prayer," so central in Orthodox experience, is pronounced by some as if it was one word, *Jesusprayer.* Jesus is regarded as a component, not as the subject or the object of the prayer. Where both types of theology agree is in assuming that we are at the end of an era, the Christian era.

A Third Way?

Is there not, in each type of theology, something that is radically missing? Face to face with the world, the one adopts an attitude of surrender, the other of escape. That is the tragedy of contemporary theology. But is there no third way? Seeking to extricate ourselves from the *impasse* brought about by these two mutually exclusive ways of looking at everything — at the world, at culture, at life, at the path to salvation — let us begin by identifying and accepting the relative truth that each of them contains. Each of them is made up of what someone in France has called *les vérités chrétiennes devenues folles*, Christian truths that have gone mad. For there *is* a Christian truth in each of them, as we can see if we bear in mind the paradoxical use of the term "world" in the New Testament. On the one hand, we are not to love the world or anything in the world (1 Jn 2:15); the world is to be transcended. Yet on the other hand it is said, "God so loved the world that he gave his only-begotten Son" (Jn 3:16). At the present moment we have some who emphasize only the first attitude to the world, we also have others who think only of the second. In certain Christian communes there is a deep and almost apocalyptic hatred for the world, with the members thinking only of the return of Christ

and even trying to predict its exact date. At the other extreme
there is the example of a highly respectable seminary in the state
of New York, which in the glorious 60s unanimously voted,
faculty and students, to close the chapel and to repent for the
useless time spent in prayer or contemplation when the world had
to be helped. Such is the antinomy: on the one side a radical "no"
and on the other radical "yes."

The Eschatological Dimension

But why have the two approaches become mutually exclusive in
this way? That is our problem. What has happened in the history
of the Church, in the Christian mind, which has led us today to
this mutual exclusion, to this polarization, not only in theology as
such but in the Christian world-view itself? The answer lies in the
abandonment, at a rather early point in the history of Christianity, of the essential eschatological dimension and foundation of
Christian faith and so of Christian theology.

It is not possible to embark here on an historical analysis of
when and how this happened. Eschatology, however, is a term so
much used and abused in modern writings, theological and non-
theological, that I would like briefly to define the exact sense in
which I am employing it. I am using it to denote the distinctive
particularity of the Christian faith, which is first of all a system of
beliefs — belief in God, belief in the saving nature of certain
historical events, and finally belief in the ultimate victory of God
in Christ and of the Kingdom of God. But at the same time as
Christians we already possess that in which we believe. The
Kingdom is still to come, and yet the Kingdom that is to come is
already in the midst of us. The Kingdom is not only something
promised, it is something of which we can taste here and now.
And so in all our preaching we are bearing witness, *martyria*, not
simply to our faith but to our possession of that in which we
believe.

Eschatology is not merely the last and strangest chapter in the treatise of theology that we have inherited from the medieval period, not merely a map of future events, telling us in advance exactly what will take place. By limiting eschatology to the last chapter of all, we have deprived all the other chapters of the eschatological character that they ought to have. Eschatology has been transposed into personal hope, personal waiting. But in reality the whole of Christian theology is eschatological, and the entire experience of life likewise. It is the very essence of the Christian faith that we live in a kind of rhythm — leaving, abandoning, denying the world, and yet at the same time always returning to it; living in time by that which is beyond time; living by that which is not yet come, but which we already know and possess.

Liturgy and Theology

One of the great sources of this abandonment of proper eschatology, of the eschatology that is fundamental to the Christian experience of the faith itself, is another divorce; the divorce between theology and the liturgical experience of the Church. Theologians have forgotten the essential principle that the *lex orandi* constitutes the *lex credendi;* they have forgotten the absolutely unique function of Christian worship within all theological speculation. So theology has come eventually to define the sacraments as no more than "channels of grace," and now modern secularized theology has gone a step further and turned them into "channels of help." But in reality the sacraments are to be seen as the *locus*, the very center of the Church's eschatological understanding and experience. The whole Liturgy is to be seen as the sacrament of the Kingdom of God, the Church is to be seen as the presence and communication of the Kingdom that is to come. The unique — I repeat, unique — function of worship in the life of the Church and in theology is to convey a sense of this

eschatological reality; and what eschatology does is to hold together things which otherwise are broken up and treated as separate events occurring at different points in a time sequence. And
when they are treated in that way, the true function of Liturgy is
forgotten.

In my own tradition, the Byzantine, this has meant, for example, the appearance of endless symbolic explanations of worship,
and so the eucharistic Liturgy that is at the heart of the Church
has been transformed in effect into a series of audio-visual aids.
Symbolism is discerned everywhere. I tried once to collect all the
meanings of the exclamation before the Creed, "The doors! The
doors!," and I found about sixteen different and mutually exclusive explanations. Or else the seven episcopal vestments were
identified with the seven gifts of the Holy Spirit. It is not that I
deny episcopacy as a source of grace, but certainly those seven
items of vesture were not originally intended to illustrate that.

In the West, on the other hand, once the eschatological dimension of the sacraments was forgotten, there developed a constant emphasis upon the notion of the Real Presence. (But is there
a presence which is not real? It could in that case only be called
absence.) Whereas the East lost sight of the true meaning of the
Liturgy through an absorption in fanciful symbolism, the West
obscured its true meaning by making a sharp distinction between
symbol and reality; and it became obsessed by questions about the
causality and precise moment of the consecration.

If we are to recover the real meaning of the Liturgy, we need to
go back, behind the commentaries with their symbolic explanations, to the actual text and celebration of the Eucharist itself. We
are to see in the Liturgy the fulfillment of the Church at the table
of the Lord in his Kingdom. The eucharistic celebration is not
something performed by the clergy for the benefit of the laity who
"attend." Rather it is the ascension of the Church to the place
where she belongs *in statu patriae.* It is also her subsequent return

to this world: her return with power to preach the Kingdom of God in the way that it was preached by Christ himself.

The same eschatological approach is to be applied to all aspects of liturgical celebration. What is Easter night? What is Pascha? We now have a historical conception of the feast: it commemorates events in the past. But for early Christian heortology it was by no means a mere commemoration or memory. It was always the entry of the Church into the lasting reality created by Christ through his death and resurrection.

Nor is the sacrament to be understood, as it has been understood for centuries, in terms of the contrast between natural and supernatural. We must return from this to the fundamental Christian dichotomy, which is between the old and the new. "Behold, I make all things new" (Rev 21:5). Notice that Christ does not say "I create new things," but "all things new." Such is the eschatological vision that should mark our eucharistic celebration on each Lord's Day. Nowadays we treat the Day of the Lord as the seventh day, the Sabbath. For the Fathers it was the eighth day, the first day of the new creation, the day on which the Church not only remembers the past but also remembers, indeed enters into, the future, the last and great day. It is the day on which the Church assembles, locking the doors, and ascends to the point at which it becomes possible to say, "Holy, holy, holy Lord God of Sabaoth, heaven and earth are full of thy glory." Tell me, what right do we have to say that? Today I read the London *Times* — a welcome change from the *New York Times* — but, whichever of them we read, does it make us say, "Heaven and earth are full of thy glory"? The world which they show us is certainly not full of the glory of God. If we make such an affirmation in the Liturgy, it is not just an expression of Christian optimism ("Onward, Christian soldiers"), but simply and solely because we have ascended to the point at which such a statement is indeed true, so that the only thing that remains for us to do is

to give thanks to God. And in that thanksgiving we are in him
and with him in his Kingdom, because there is now nothing else
left, because that is where our ascension has already led us.

Created, Fallen, Redeemed

It is here, in the liturgical experience and the liturgical testimony
which enables us to sing, "Heaven and earth are full of thy glory";
it is here that we restore, or at least have the possibility of restoring, the essential Christian vision of the world, and therefore an
agenda for theology. In this vision or agenda there are three
elements, three fundamental acclamations of faith, which we are
to hold together in unity.

First, God has created the world; we are God's creatures. To
say this is not to involve ourselves in questions about Darwin and
the biblical creation stories, a dispute still very much alive in parts
of America today. That is not at all the real point. To claim that
we are God's creation is to affirm that God's voice is constantly
speaking within us and saying to us, "And God saw everything
that he had made, and behold, it was very good" (Gen 1:31). The
Fathers state that even the devil is good by nature and evil only
through the misuse of his free will.

Then there is a second element, inseparable from the first: this
world is fallen — fallen in its entirety; it has become the kingdom
of the prince of this world. The Puritan world-view, so prevalent
within the American society in which I live, assumes that tomato
juice is always good and that alcohol is always bad; in effect,
tomato juice is not fallen. Similarly the television advertisements
tell us, "Milk is natural"; in other words, it also is not fallen. But
in reality tomato juice and milk are equally part of the fallen
world, along with everything else.

All is created good; all is fallen; and finally — this is our third
"fundamental acclamation" — all is redeemed. It is redeemed
through the incarnation, the cross, the resurrection and ascension

of Christ, and through the gift of the Spirit at Pentecost. Such is the triune intuition that we receive from God with gratitude and joy: our vision of the world as created, fallen, redeemed. Here is our theological agenda, our key to all the problems which today trouble the world.

The Joy of the Kingdom

We cannot answer the world's problems by adopting towards them an attitude either of surrender or of escape. We can answer the world's problems only by changing those problems, by understanding them in a different perspective. What is required is a return on our part to that source of energy, in the deepest sense of the word, which the Church possessed when it was conquering the world. What the Church brought into the world was not certain ideas applicable simply to human needs, but first of all the truth, the righteousness, the joy of the Kingdom of God.

The *joy* of the Kingdom: it always worries me that, in the multi-volume systems of dogmatic theology that we have inherited, almost every term is explained and discussed except the one word with which the Christian Gospel opens and closes. "For behold, I bring you tidings of great joy" (Lk 2:10) — so the Gospel begins, with the message of the angels. "And they worshipped him and returned to Jerusalem with great joy" (Lk 24:52) — so the Gospel ends. There is in fact no theological definition of joy. For we cannot define that sense of joy which no one can take away from us, and at this point all definitions are silent. Yet only if this experience of the joy of the Kingdom in all its fullness is again placed at the center of theology, does it become possible for theology to deal once more with creation in its true cosmic dimensions, with the historic reality of the fight between the Kingdom of God and the kingdom of the prince of this world, and finally with redemption as the plenitude, the victory and the presence of God, who becomes all in all things.

What is needed is not more liturgical piety. On the contrary, one of the greatest enemies of the Liturgy is liturgical piety. The Liturgy is not to be treated as an aesthetic experience or a therapeutic exercise. Its unique function is to reveal to us the Kingdom of God. This is what we commemorate eternally. The remembrance, the *anamnesis* of the Kingdom is the source of everything else in the Church. It is this that theology strives to bring to the world. And it comes even to a "post-Christian" world as the gift of healing, of redemption and of joy.

7

The Liturgical Revival and the Orthodox Church

Since the title of my address is somewhat ambiguous, I must define what I mean by "The Liturgical Revival and the Orthodox Church."[1] Why was an Orthodox priest invited to speak at a western liturgical conference, and in what capacity? There are many Orthodox who think that the Orthodox must always teach. Yet in my own studies in liturgics, I have found that much inspiration and many important insights have come from western liturgical achievements. Therefore, it is not because of a "secret" that we must proclaim and share with others that I am here.

It is true, however, that the Orthodox Church has always attracted the attention of all those who are active in matters liturgical. They have a natural sympathy for the East, and this for several reasons. Dom Olivier Rousseau, the Roman Catholic historian of the Liturgical Movement, wrote recently that the Eastern Church is the liturgical Church *par excellence*.[2] He even goes so far as to say that the Orthodox Church needs no liturgical revival because it has preserved intact the great liturgical prayer of the early Church. This, I think, is an overstatement. We all need a liturgical revival, and the "liturgical" Churches may be in need of it even more than the non-liturgical ones.

But it is true that the great names of St Basil and St John Chrysostom are not to be *discovered* in our tradition. They are

1. From *The Eucharist and Liturgical Renewal*, ed. by Massey Hamilton Shepherd. Copyright © 1960 by Oxford University Press, Inc. Reprinted by permission.
2. *The Progress of the Liturgy*, Newman Press, 1951, pp. 139ff.

there. Our liturgy is still deeply "patristic," and from this point of
view the western Liturgical Movement has been in many respects
a *rediscovery* of some ideas and principles which in the eastern
tradition are "natural." Take, for example, Dom Odo Casel and
some other leaders of the Liturgical Movement in Europe. They
all attempt to rediscover the patristic idea of the liturgy and
therefore are so deeply interested in the unbroken liturgical tradition of the Eastern Church.

There exist, of course, less valid reasons for this interest in the
eastern liturgy. Some people love it for its liturgical "exoticism"
and "Orientalism," for its being different from the western patterns. This is, of course, a superficial approach. The real Liturgical
Movement did not grow out of a "rubricistic" curiosity or an
interest in liturgical colors. It began with a strange shock experienced by some Christians when, after centuries and centuries,
they realized of a sudden that Christ really said, "Take, eat, this is
my Body" — and it is not taken, not eaten. Or, as a Roman
Catholic priest wrote, "I was a priest for forty years before I knew
what Easter meant in the life of the Church." And this is why we
all need a liturgical revival.

It so happened that in the West the liturgical revival was first
of all a return to the *corporate* idea of worship. The underlying
ecclesiological principle was that of the Church as the Body of
Christ; and the whole movement took mainly that direction. And
probably it is one of the most needed, most essential aspects and
merits of the Liturgical Movement. But from the Orthodox point
of view (and this is what justifies my appearance here), there are
also other dimensions of the liturgy that must be rediscovered,
brought back into our corporate experience of worship. To focus
your attention on them is my purpose in this short paper.

At the beginning of my liturgical studies, I of necessity read the
various theological and liturgical explanations of the Eucharist. I
found that virtually all of them were *symbolic* explanations. Au-

thor after author, theologian after theologian, was making the same affirmation: that the Divine Liturgy is a *symbolic representation of the earthly life of Christ.* The Entrance with the Gospel, which we have at the beginning of the rite, "represents" Christ going to preach, and the altar boy who precedes him with the candle is the "symbol" of John the Baptist — and so on, through the whole service. If you take a Byzantine classic, Nicholas Cabasilas' *Explanation of the Divine Liturgy,* you will see that every detail of the service has a symbolic explanation, and sometimes not one but as many as four or five. Thus the exclamation: "The doors, the doors!" can mean at the same time that the doors of our hearts must be closed to earthly temptations and open to the spiritual reality, or then that the doors of the Church are open to those who believe and closed to the heretics. But the partisans of "symbolism" are never embarrassed by contradictions.

And yet, all theologians agree that within this "symbolic" liturgy, at one precise moment, the "symbolism" disappears and is replaced by "realism." When dealing with the transformation of the bread and wine into the Body and Blood of Christ, the term "symbolic" is out of order and sounds heretical. We have thus a long "symbolic" representation, one point of which and one point only ceases to be symbolic and becomes "real presence." And because of this, the theologians, leaving the symbolic framework to liturgiologists, concentrate all their attention upon this precise moment, trying to define and to express its precision. *When* does it happen, *how* does it happen, and *what* exactly is it that happens?

The long controversies about the Eucharist were always attempts to reach precise answers to these and similar questions. I am not quite certain that the type of precision achieved in these elaborations is adequate to its object. But it is clear that we have, as a result of it, two different ways of looking at the Eucharist, ways which are by no means connected with each other. The *liturgical* approach (in the old acceptance of the term "liturgical") is concerned with symbolism in all its possible variations. The *theological* approach isolates the *quid* of the liturgy from its liturgical framework (thought of as precisely a framework, useful and beautiful but not essentially necessary), and deals exclusively with the question of the *validity*. i.e., the minimum of conditions required for the Eucharist. In my opinion, the time has come for *liturgical theology*, or, in other terms, for a theology that would respect the liturgy as we receive it from tradition, and a liturgiology whose aim would once more be the formulation and explication of the *lex orandi* as the *lex credendi* of the Church.

In this approach, the question, which for a long time has been not only central but almost the only question in all Eucharistic theology — namely, *what* happens to the elements (and the *how* and the *when*) — must not precede, but must follow another basic question. *What happens to the Church in the Eucharist?* For it is only when this question is asked that certain of the affirmations made by the Eastern Church can be understood: the affirmation — for example, that the very ideas of a moment of consecration and also of the *essential* and the *non-essential* acts in the liturgy, etc., are not adequate — should not be applied in Eucharistic theology; nor should the affirmation that it is the *Epiclesis,* the invocation of the Holy Spirit, that constitutes the real "form" of the Eucharistic sacrament. At the time they were made, they expressed the opposition of the Orthodox Church to some western theories rather than a consistent sacramental doctrine. But, as we move toward a liturgical theology, they acquire their full meaning and become the starting points of a fuller theological understanding of the Eucharist.

In this short presentation, I want to take you through a quick analysis of the Eucharist, as it is celebrated in the Orthodox Church. We know that the basic "shape of the liturgy," to use the phrase of Gregory Dix, is common to all liturgical traditions. The Byzantine liturgy, however — and in spite of a certain enmity for it of the same Dom Dix — remains, in my opinion, a unique theological and liturgical synthesis. It could perhaps be purified of certain elements, introduced into it under the influence of the above-mentioned symbolism, and also of some "Orientalisms" (for one has to distinguish between the "Eastern" and the "Oriental," when one deals with Orthodox worship). But even as it stands now it is still the best and the fullest expression of Catholic worship. This is why I suggest that we analyze it briefly, and perhaps some of the questions which I raised at the beginning of this paper will at least receive a preliminary and tentative answer.

Let me stress once more that the very spirit of liturgy, as the Eastern Church understands it, excluded the distinction between the "important" and the "unimportant" moments or acts. To Orthodox young people who often ask me, "Father, what is the most important moment of the liturgy?", I always give the same answer: "The whole liturgy." And I add some illustration such as this: "When you want water to boil and therefore consider that the important moment is when it finally boils, you still know that you will not reach this point unless you first let the water warm up." The Eucharist can be viewed as a journey or a *procession*, which leads us ultimately to the final destination, but in which every stage is equally important.

This procession actually begins when Christians leave their homes for the church. They leave their life in this present world, and whether they have to drive fifteen miles or just walk a few blocks, a *liturgical act* is already taking place, and this act is the very condition of everything else that is to happen. They are now on their way to *constitute the Church*, for their gathering together results not in a mere sum of so many individuals, but in the *ecclesia*, the Church. This is the first *transformation* that takes place at the Liturgy, and it is not a symbolic one. It is the first in a long sequence of transformations which all together constitute the Liturgy, the Sacrament of the Church, its fulfillment.

The minister of this transformation, as well as of all the others, is the priest. Without his coming, the group would remain just another human group and, however spiritual or even holy, not the Church. But the celebrant stands in the center, and his vestments and insignia express first of all and above everything else his relation to the body of the Church as its head: *totus Christus, caput et corpus.*

Then comes the initial acclamation: "Blessed is the kingdom of the Father, the Son, and the Holy Spirit." From the beginning the destination is announced: the journey is to the Kingdom. This is where we are going, and again — not symbolically, not psychologically — but indeed, really and "ontologically." The congregation answers *Amen*, and it is probably one of the most important liturgical terms, for it expresses the agreement of the Church to follow Christ in His Ascension to His Father.

During the first part of the Liturgy, the bishop stands in the center of the church. He has not approached the altar. He has not entered the sanctuary. He is in the center of his flock — the Pastor, the leader, the head of the body. And the Liturgy begins by the common prayers and supplications of the assembly, a common and joyful praise. This joyful character of the Eucharistic gathering must be stressed. For the medieval emphasis on the Cross, the sacrificial character of the Eucharist, while not a wrong one, is certainly one-sided. The Liturgy is, first of all, the Paschal gathering of those who are to meet the risen Lord and to enter with Him into His Kingdom.

Then comes the *Entrance.* If, from its usual symbolic explanation, we go back to its real meaning, we discover that it is not a symbolic, but a *real* entrance. It is the real approaching of the altar, a real entrance into the sanctuary, which in liturgy *re-presents* (makes present) the Kingdom. It is the place of Divine Presence, the place where the Table of the Lord is being prepared for us, where once more we are invited to partake of the banquet of the Kingdom. It is therefore a solemn Entrance. And when the bishop enters the Royal Door of the Iconostasis, in him we all, the whole body, perform the same entrance, for he is the head of the body.

At this point appears the liturgical theme of *Angels*, and we must consider it briefly. It is noteworthy that in the Byzantine liturgical synthesis the "terms of reference" of the Entrance are precisely the angelic powers. We sing the angelic *Trisagion*: "Holy God, Holy Mighty, Holy Immortal"; and the prayer which the priest reads after he has approached the altar begins by a mention of the angels ("O holy God ... who art praised with thrice-holy voice of the Seraphim, glorified by the Cherubim, and adored by all hosts of heaven," etc.). The angels are not here for decoration, or because it is nice and inspiring to mention the Seraphim and the Cherubim from time to time. The liturgical function of this mention (and this also is true of the *Sanctus*) is to certify that the Church has entered its heavenly dimension, has *ascended into heaven*. It indicates that we are now at the Throne of God, where the angels eternally sing "Holy, Holy, Holy."

Thus, following the first step — our transformation into the Church — the Liturgy now has achieved its second step: the entrance into the *aeon* to which the Church continually belongs. The priest, who now stands before the altar, says "O Holy *God*." He gives God His *real* Name, and worships His real, heavenly essence, because "holiness" means, on the one hand, that God is the Absolutely Other, and, on the other hand, that He is the desire of all our desire, the goal and fulfillment of our life. And then while the choir sings — slowly, solemnly — the *Trisagion* Hymn, the procession moves further. The celebrant goes behind the altar (the "high place" or the "throne" in Byzantine liturgical terminology) and, for the first time, turns back and faces the people. Now he himself is being transformed. For up to this moment he was the one who *led* the Church in its ascension to the heavenly altar; but when now he turns his face to the people and, raising his hand, says, "Peace be with you all," the movement has reached its goal and the Presence of God *given* us. He spoke *for* the Church, and now he speaks *to* the Church. He re-presented the Church before God, and now he re-presents God to the Chruch. And fulfilling thus his ministry, he re-presents Christ, the Head of the new humanity and the One who reveals God, the Emmanuel.

For a long time the movement of the Liturgy was explained as a movement *downwards*: as grace which the priest takes "from heaven" and brings down to us. It seems to me that such an explanation must be completed by its opposite. It is not God who is being taken from heaven, placed on our altars, and then put into the mouths of men. It is the Church that is being lifted up and ascends to heaven. A very important liturgical category is that of Christ's Ascension, and we must not forget that the first manual of liturgics, the Epistle to the Hebrews, was written precisely in terms of Ascension.

The Entrance is thus the ascension of the Church to where it belongs. Although it is still in this *aeon*, in this world and its time, it is essential for the Church to leave "this world" and to recover regularly this dimension of Ascension; and this is done in and through the Liturgy. And it is in this dimension of the Kingdom that we listen again to the Word of God. In our Church, the Epistle is read by a layman, the Gospel by the deacon, and the Sermon is preached by the priest. All Orders of the Church take part in the "liturgy of the Word," the text of Scripture given to the whole Church. But it belongs to the priest to perform the Sacrament of the Word, and this is the real meaning of the *liturgical Sermon*. In it the "text" (the human word of Scripture) is *transformed* into the Word of God to be given us. It was Origen who said that there were two communions at the Liturgy: the first, the Word of God; the second the Body and Blood.

With the liturgical Sermon, the first part of the Liturgy — the

Synaxis — comes to its end, and we move into the Eucharistic sacrifice. Much has been written about the sacrificial character of the Eucharist, yet the issue still remains confused. Perhaps a very simple liturgical approach can help here.

First, we offer to God some very simple elements of our food: some bread and some wine. As you probably know, the Eastern Church uses the leavened bread for its *prosphora*; so it is really what we eat at home that is being offered to God as our sacrifice. And a good liturgical and Biblical study would clearly show that this offering of food means, first of all, that we are *offering ourselves*. Food is not only the symbol of life, but being the condition of life, being that which becomes our body, food *is* life and therefore *our* life — we ourselves. The first and real sacrifice is, thus, the sacrifice of the Church itself. But (and this "but" is very important) it is a *sacrifice in Christ*. It is not a new sacrifice because it is the sacrifice of the Church, and the Church is the Body of Christ. From the first moment of the Liturgy, Christ is not only the One who *accepts* the sacrifice, but in the words of one of the liturgical prayers, the One who also *offers*. All our sacrifices — and a Christian is by his very nature a living sacrifice to God — converge at the one and unique sacrifice, full and perfect, that of Christ's humanity, which He offered to God and in which we are included through our membership in the Church.

We are offering this sacrifice not because God needs it, but because Christ's sacrifice is the essence, the condition of our being in Him. The Orthodox theology, when contemplating this sacrifice, stresses love in it rather than "satisfaction" or expiation. To be a sacrificial Being belongs to the very essence of the Son of God even before Incarnation and Redemption. For *sacrifice*, before it becomes sacrifice for something, is the natural and necessary expression of love. Christ's whole life is a sacrifice because it is a perfect life made of love and love alone. And since it is His own life that He gives us (Christ in us, we in Christ) our life is also a sacrifice. Our sacrifice in Him, His sacrifice in us. And thus again, it is a real, not a symbolical sacrifice; yet not a new one, but always the same, the one that he gave us, into which he has taken us. The Church, being the Body of Christ, is itself a sacrificial being because it knows that the essence of man's life — as seen in His Humanity — is to *go to God.* And this going determines the movement of sacrifice. All this is expressed in the Prayer of the Cherubic Hymn: "Thou are the One who offers and the One who art offered, and Thou receivest and thou art distributed."

It is a wonderful identification with Christ. We offer *our* sacrifice to God the Father, and yet we have nothing to offer but Christ Himself; for He is our life and offering. Sacrificing our life, we offer Him. Our Eucharist is His Eucharist, and He also *is* our Eucharist.

After the Creed and the Kiss of Love ("Let us love one another that in one accord we may confess," etc.), we are ready for the great Eucharistic prayer, which from time immemorial constituted the very essence of the whole Eucharist. Eucharist means thanksgiving. *But how is thanksgiving related to consecration?* To this question the various theological theories give no satisfactory answer. Under their influence the thanksgiving element of the Eucharistic prayer was called *Preface.* Yet a preface is usually not something too important. Do we not sometimes read the preface of a book after we have read the book itself? But in the Eucharist it is precisely this "Preface" that makes everything else, including the consecration and the transformation of the elements, possible; and we understand why thanksgiving is the *only* way to that transformation and so understand the whole meaning of the Eucharist.

For centuries the emphasis was laid on the "night in which He was betrayed" — on the bloody aspect of His Sacrifice. But in liturgical tradition, which no sacramental theory has been able to break, the prayer begins with a solemn thanksgiving. And Christ also began His sacrifice with a thanksgiving: "And when He had given thanks, He broke it . . . and gave it."

The reason for this, however, forgotten as it may be, is a simple one. Eucharist, thanksgiving, is the state of the innocent man, the state of paradise. Before sin, man's life was eucharistic, for "eucharist" is the only relationship between God and man which transcends and transforms man's created condition. This condition is that of a total, an absolute dependence. Dependence is slavery. But when this dependence is accepted and lived as "eucharist," i.e. as love, thanksgiving, adoration, it is no longer dependence; it is an attitude of freedom, a state in which God is the *content* of life. Eucharist, thus, is the only state of innocence, and Adam and Eve had it and it was the divine image in them.

Then man lost it. There are many theories of what original sin was, but in terms of liturgical theology one can say that the original sin was the loss of that eucharistic state. The loss of the real life, which is eucharistic life, was the loss of the life in love and communion. The Old Testament reflects an endless attempt to recover "eucharist," but no one can offer it fully because "eucharist" is the state, the attitude, and the act of the innocent man in whom life, meaning of life, and fullness of life are one and the same thing. It was a certain experience of life that man had lost — the eucharistic experience. But then salvation could be nothing else but the restoration of life as "eucharist." It was restored in Christ. His whole life, and He Himself, was a perfect Eucharist, a full and perfect offering to God. Thus the Eucharist was restored to man.

Therefore, when the priest proclaims: "Let us give thanks unto the Lord!" — we realize that the whole movement, the whole procession was necessary for it was achieving the state of innocence, making the Eucharist possible. And now once more man stands before God restored to his pristine beauty, innocent, perfect, the very image of God's love. He has nothing to ask for, for

he has already received "grace upon grace" and has been admitted
to the Kingdom. What does then remain?

When the movement, the procession, reaches its goal, and all
prayers have been said and everything that exists has been com-
memorated, there remains but one ultimate reality — the Eucharist. This is why the whole movement comes to this last and
unique exhortation: *eucharistesomen* ("Let us give thanks!").

But we know that no one can say this, no one can offer this but
Christ. It was His unique Eucharist that has led us up to this
point; we were taken into His Ascension, His *passage* to His
Father. We were offering in Him. And now we realize that the
content of our Eucharist is Christ again, for there is nothing else
that we can offer to God. It is not a new Eucharist. We are
accepted into the eternal Eucharist which Christ offers and of
which He is the offering. He stands there — in heaven —
eternally. He is the end, the *Eschaton*, and our Eucharist is thus
not in the past, the present, or the future. It is the *Eschaton*, in the
glorified Christ.

Now we can understand the relation between the Eucharist
and the consecration. We can say that what "happens" to the
elements of bread and wine happens precisely because of our
being in the Eucharist, in the *Eschaton*. It happens because we are
in the *aeon*, in which the transformation is not a mere "miracle,"
but somehow the natural consequence of our ascension into it.
The food (the life!) which God gives us is once more He Himself.

Of this fulfillment of the Eucharistic procession, of our "ar-
rival" and acceptance in the Kingdom, the *Sanctus* is the expression and sign. We sing the angelic hymn because in Christ we
have entered heaven. And having entered there, we offer Christ as
our Eucharist, because "by nature" we have no admittance, because only in Him has this become possible. Hence — the *Anamnesis*, the recapitulation of how all this happened, of the whole
economy of salvation. This is what we "remember" in heaven,

before the throne of God, because there is nothing else that man could remember and offer.

And then in this remembrance we come to that night, to that Supper, and we repeat what He said then: "Take, eat ... drink ... do this." Having reached this point, the movement of the Eucharist is reversed. Until now, we were ascending, going up, moving toward God. But now once more He comes to us, as in Paradise, to feed us with the new life of the new *aeon*, to fulfill His communion with us. This moment of reversion is the consecration. It is the sign that our offering has been accepted, that our Eucharist has been fulfilled, that we have entered into the eternal Eucharist of Jesus Christ.

The Orthodox Church has always affirmed the necessity of the *Epiclesis*, the invocation of the Holy Spirit, for the consecration, i.e. the transformation of bread and wine into the Body and Blood of Christ. This affirmation is still the object of a heated controversy, both historical and theological. But one has to go beyond the purely historical or purely scholastic argumentation and discover the true significance of the Holy Spirit in the Eucharist. His coming, His action, means always the fulfillment of the *Eschaton*, the coming of the new *aeon*, the last Day. And in the Eucharist, which is the Sacrament of the Church, the *Epiclesis* means that the ultimate transformation has become possible only because of our entrance into heaven, our being in the *Eschaton*, in the day of Pentecost which is the day after and beyond the seventh day, the day which is beyond time, the day of the Spirit.

The last action of the Eucharist is the participation in the eschatological banquet of the Kingdom, the communion. Its importance has been duly stressed in the Liturgical Movement. But I must again and again point to its meaning as our participation in *the world to come*. It is our communion in the Spirit, or, in other terms, in the *aeon* of the Kingdom.

Then the priest says: "Let us depart in peace." This does not mean, of course, that having accomplished our religious duty we can now simply go home and "relax." How can one *return* from the Kingdom? And yet we are given this order, and it is precisely as an order that those words must be understood. This gives the Eucharist its last dimension — that of *Mission.*

We were first ordered to leave the world and forget it: "Let us put aside all earthly care." And this was the condition of our ascension into the *Parousia,* the Presence of Christ, of our communion in the Spirit. But now that "we have seen the true light and partaken of the Holy Spirit," now that we have fully realized the Church as being not of this world, we are sent back into the world, and the eschatological sacrament becomes the very condition of our work and life in it. For the sacrament has made us capable of bearing testimony to the Kingdom and life eternal. "We have seen, we have touched, we have been *there* ..." And we can thus be responsible Christians, for we can now refer everything to that which happened to us — to that eucharistic ascension on Mount Tabor. It is here that we find the guiding principle for our Christian action in the world. By transforming the Church into what it is, the Eucharist makes it capable of being the real center and heart of its mission to the world.

The Eucharist is thus the Sacrament of the Church, transforming us again and again into *membra Christi.* It is then the Sacrament of the real Sacrifice, in which our sacrifice becomes that of Christ. And it is finally the Sacrament of the *Parousia,* the Presence of Christ and of His Kingdom. These three aspects of the Eucharist must be always kept together, and it is one of the main tasks of the Liturgical Movement to recover the eschatological dimension of the liturgy. The real life of the Church is revealed and fulfilled every Sunday. We partake of the *Eschaton* and to it we can witness in our life in this world. If we realize this, the Liturgical Movement acquires a real sense of purpose.

8

Symbols and Symbolism in the Byzantine Liturgy:
Liturgical Symbols and Their Theological Interpretation

Whatever else a reasonably educated westerner may or may not know about Byzantium, chances are that he has at least heard about the "rich symbolism" of Byzantine worship.[1] Indeed the terms "symbols" and "symbolism" have, for all practical purposes, become almost synonymous with the Byzantine liturgy — a cliché whose self-evidence requires no further explanation. My purpose in this paper is to try to show that, contrary to that cliché, the Byzantine liturgical symbolism confronts us with problems important not only for the understanding of the Byzantine liturgy itself but of the Byzantine religious mind in general. It is an attempt to outline, be it only tentatively, the problem as I see it, and to indicate, of necessity in very general terms, the possible ways towards its solution.

Taken at its face value, the symbolism usually ascribed to the Byzantine liturgy as its essential element seems to present no great problem. There exists a substantial number of Byzantine and post-Byzantine — Greek, Russian, Serbian, etc. — commentaries in which all liturgical acts, as well as the liturgy in its totality, are interpreted as being above all *symbolic representations*, i.e., as acts "representing," "signifying," and thus "symbolizing," *something*

1. Originally published in D. Constantelos, ed., *Orthodox Theology and Diakonia,* Festschrift Iakovos, Brookline, MA, Hellenic College Press, 1981, pp. 91-102.

else, be it an event of the past, an idea, or a theological affirmation. This symbolism, common to all Byzantine worship, is especially elaborate in commentaries on the central act of that worship — the celebration of the Eucharist. The divine liturgy is for all commentators virtually a symbolic representation of the life and ministry of Christ from His birth in Bethlehem to His glorious ascension to heaven. The *prothesis*, i.e., the ritual preparation of the Eucharistic gifts of bread and wine, is the symbol of Christ's birth; the so-called "Little Entrance" or the Introit, the symbol of His manifestation to the world; the "Great Entrance," or the procession with the gifts to the altar, the symbol of Christ's burial and of His triumphant entrance into Jerusalem,[2] etc. These symbolic explanations differ from one another only in the degree of their complexity and elaboration, of their attention to details, of their extension even to secondary and minor rites. They also may occasionally contradict one another; the same act, as I have just mentioned for the Great Entrance, can have two or even more rather incompatible symbolic meanings. On the whole, however, such symbolism remains simple as to its nature and function. Symbol here is reduced to an illustration whose purpose can be termed pedagogic or educational. Why is it, to paraphrase one of the popular Byzantine commentators, Germanus of Constantinople, that the bishop takes no part in the initial acts of the divine liturgy and lets the priest perform them? Because the priest symbolizes Saint John the Baptist and it is fitting for him to perform those acts which symbolize the time preceding Christ's manifestation. And likewise, the same is true in the entire liturgy. The symbolic meanings, I repeat, may change, overlap one another, be more or less elaborate, but their nature remains the same. On the level of celebration, of "externals," the divine liturgy is above all a sacred play, a representation in the usual meaning of that word.

2. Cf. R. Taft, *The Great Entrance, A History of the Transfer of Gifts and Other Pre-Anaphoral Rites of the Liturgy of St John Chrysostom,* Orientalia Christiana Analecta 200, Rome, 1975.

And it is obviously this illustrative symbolism, it is the "dramatic" character of the Byzantine liturgy that is being referred to in the descriptions and definitions of it as "symbolic," as endowed with a particularly "rich" symbolism.

And yet it is here, it is precisely in considering this seemingly traditional illustrative symbolism that we encounter our first difficulty and thus the first dimension of the problem I announced earlier. The difficulty lies in a simple and easily verifiable fact: the absence of virtually any reference to such symbols and symbolic meanings in the liturgy itself, and this means primarily in the prayers in which the different rites and liturgical actions are given their verbal expression and thus their meaning.

Let us take, as examples, the rites I have already mentioned; the so-called "Little Entrance" and the "Great Entrance," both of which have always been privileged focuses of the illustrative symbolism. I have said already that the Little Entrance, which in present usage is a solemn procession of the clergy carrying the Gospel from the sanctuary and back to the sanctuary, is interpreted in all commentaries as representing or symbolizing Christ's coming to the people and the inauguration by Him of His preaching ministry. But if we consult the liturgy itself and, first of all, the prayers accompanying this entrance and thus "expressing" its meaning, nowhere shall we find the slightest indication that it has anything to do with the meaning ascribed to it in liturgical commentaries. In the first place, there exists an obvious contradiction between the rite referred to in all prayers as "entrance" and its interpretation in all commentaries as an "exodus," as Christ's "going out" to preach. Then, the Gospel in this rite is carried not by the priest, who symbolizes Christ, but by the deacon, whose symbolic function, according to the commentaries, is usually that of angel or apostle. As to the prayers accompanying this rite, their consistent term of reference is not the manifestation of Christ but the Church joining the angelic powers and their eternal praise.

Thus, the Prayer of Entrance: "... grant that with our entrance there may be the entrance of the holy angels ..."; thus, the Prayer of the Trisagion: "O holy God ... who are hymned by the Seraphim with the thrice-holy cry, and glorified by the Cherubim ..."; thus, finally, the Trisagion itself, the hymn of the entrance which is clearly derived from the "Holy, Holy, Holy" of Isaiah's vision. Of this angelic symbolism I shall speak later. At this point it suffices to say that in terms of the liturgical *ordo* itself, of rites and prayers alike, the meaning of the Little Entrance is that of *our*, i.e. the Church's, entrance to heaven, into the eternal glorification of God by the angelic hosts.

We find the same discrepancy between the illustrative symbolism on the one hand and the liturgy itself on the other hand when we consider the Great Entrance. The solemn transfer of the Eucharistic gifts from the table of *prothesis* to the altar became, at an early date, the object of several symbolic interpretations — the most popular of which saw in it the symbol of Christ's burial. And it must be said that in the present *ordo* of the Great Entrance there are some references to this symbolism of burial. But they are found only in what Father Taft, in his admirable monograph, calls "secondary formulae" — the reading of the celebrant, after placing the gifts on the altar, of the hymns of Good Friday — "Noble Joseph..." etc., the image of the *Threnos*, the burial of Christ, first on the *aer*— the veil covering the gifts — and then on the *eiliton*, or the *antimension*, etc. These are indeed secondary rites and representations, and not only because of their late appearance in the liturgy, but also because they clearly constitute a kind of alien theme within the essential and organic sequence of rites and prayers forming the Great Entrance. The real meaning of that sequence is expressed in the two Prayers of the Faithful which precede the entrance of the gifts, and in the Prayer of the Proskomide which concludes that entrance and which even in today's *euchologia* is called "the prayer of the priest after he has placed the holy gifts on the altar." And in none of these prayers, whether in the liturgy of St John Chrysostom or in that of St Basil, do we find any reference to the burial of Christ, or, for that matter, to any event of His life. In all of them the transfer of gifts and their being placed on the altar is expressed in sacrificial terms, but again, as *our* sacrifice, as a sacrifice of praise, which we ask God to receive "from the hands of us sinners..." If it is a symbol, it certainly does not belong to the category of illustrative symbolism.

Such examples could be multiplied *ad infinitum* and they all point to the same evidence; that of radical discrepancy between the *lex orandi* as expressed and embodied in the liturgy itself and its symbolic interpretation, which nevertheless is commonly held to be an organic part of the Orthodox tradition and which permeates the manuals of liturgics as well as the common piety of churchgoers. Even to question it is, in the eyes of an overwhelming majority, tantamount to subversion and heresy. And thus, the inescapable question is: how, why and when did this illustrative symbolism appear and what does it mean in the history of the Byzantine religious mind?

In his very valuable and in many ways truly pioneering book, *The Byzantine Commentaries of the Divine Liturgy Between the Seventh and the Fifteenth Centuries*, Father René Bornert answers some of these questions.[3] His conclusions, based on a very thorough study of available sources, can be summarized as follows. The origin of the symbolic interpretation of the liturgy is to be found in the catechetical instructions given in preparation for baptism to the newly converted. This pre- and post-baptismal initiation, in turn, reflects and is patterned after scriptural exegesis, the interpretation of the Holy Scripture as it develops in two main traditions — the Alexandrian, with its emphasis on *theoria*, the spiritual or anagogical meaning of Scripture, and the Antiochian, with its affirmation of *historia*, the sequence of events re-

---

3. R. Bornert, *Les Commentaires byzantins de la divine liturgie du VIIe au XVe siècle,"* Archives de l'Orient Chrétien, Paris, 1966.

vealed as history of salvation. What is important, however, is that
in both traditions the liturgy, similar in this to Scripture, is
considered as a source of gnosis, the knowledge of God revealing
Himself in His saving acts. The Alexandrian catechetical tradition
is represented by Origen, Saint Gregory of Nyssa, and, later, by
Pseudo-Dionysius; the Antiochian, by the catechetical instructions of Saint Cyril of Jerusalem, Saint John Chrysostom, and
Theodore of Mopsuestia.

Then, "at the dawn of the Byzantine and medieval era," writes
Father Bornert, "we see in the East, as well as in the West, the
blossoming of a new literary genre: the *mystical commentary*." Its
purpose and task are different from those of the catechetical
instruction. The latter was aimed at the catechumens, and its
purpose was to prepare the future members of the Church for
proper participation in the Church's worship. The mystical commentary is addressed to the faithful. Its purpose is to explain the
mysterion, the spiritual meaning, the spiritual reality, hidden, yet
present behind the visible signs and rites of the liturgy. If the
catechetical instructions deal almost exclusively with the rites of
initiation, the mystagogical commentary is focused primarily on
the divine liturgy. The best, one can say the classical, example of
this mystagogical approach to and interpretation of the liturgy is
the *Mystagogia* of the great Byzantine theologian of the seventh
century, Saint Maximus the Confessor. Even if many, if not the
majority, of his symbolic explanations of the liturgy have their
antecedents in earlier documents, it is he who by integrating them
into a consistent whole prepares in many ways the ultimate triumph of symbolism as the content of both the form and the spirit
of the Byzantine liturgy, and thus as, in fact, the unique key to its
understanding.

Thus, by tracing the history of the present illustrative symbolism back to the mystagogical commentary and through it to the
catechetical instruction, we have the answer to our first question

— that about the causes and the factors which prepared its ultimate identification with the Church's *lex orandi*. And yet the main question remains unanswered, and Father Bornert not only does not answer it in his, I repeat, excellent book, but, in fact, seems unaware of its very existence. It is the question stemming from what I called the discrepancy between the symbolic interpretation of the liturgy and the liturgy itself; between the meaning imposed, so to speak, on the liturgy by its commentators and the meaning implied in the liturgical texts, and more widely, in the very *ordo*, the structure of the liturgical celebration.

Now if a scholar like Father Bornert seems simply to ignore this question it is because he, together with many others, bases his whole investigation on the presupposition of an organic continuity between the different stages in the development of the Byzantine liturgical experience; of that which, for lack of a better term, I call "liturgical piety." And yet, it is precisely this continuity, the continuity not of the liturgy itself, of its basic structure or *ordo*, but of its comprehension by both theology and piety that, I am convinced, must be questioned and re-evaluated if we are to progress in our understanding of the Byzantine religious mind and experience.

Simply stated, my thesis is that there is an organic continuity in the liturgy itself, that is, in its meaning as revealed in its fundamental *ordo* or structure; and there is a discontinuity in the comprehension, i.e., in the understanding and, deeper, in the experience of the liturgy by the ecclesial society at large.

It is obviously impossible within the limits of this paper to go into any detailed elaboration of this thesis, with which in a more detailed manner I dealt in my book, *Introduction to Liturgical Theology*.[4] If I state it here in its most general form, it is because

4. A. Schmemann, *Introduction to Liturgical Theology*, London, 1966. Cf. also my essay: "Sacrament and Symbol" in *For the Life of the World*, Crestwood, NY, 1973, pp. 135-51.

it will help us, I am sure, better to understand the whole problem
of Byzantine liturgical symbolism and its development. For, when
applied to that development, the notion of discontinuity means
first of all the discontinuity among the various understandings of
the symbol itself, of its very nature and function in the liturgy.
Thus, the word "symbol" and all its semantic derivatives, "represents," "signifies," etc., means one thing in the theological vocabulary of a Saint Maximus the Confessor and a substantially
different thing in the explanation of the divine liturgy by Germanus of Constantinople (eighth century), an explanation which
Father Bornert rightly defines as the "quasi official or at least the
most commonly accepted" interpretation, and which without any
doubt served as the main source for the later illustrative symbolism."[5] The discontinuity, the difference here is, above all, of a
theological nature. It is a difference between two understandings
of the symbol in its relationship to theology.

Without going into the details of Saint Maximus' theology,
one can safely say that for him the symbol (as well as the other
more or less equivalent terms, *typos* and *eikon*) are inseparable
from, and for all practical purposes, subordinated to the central
notion of mystery, *mysterion*, which, at least in its application to
the liturgy, refers to the mystery of Christ and to His saving
ministry. It is the mystery of the Incarnation and of the redemption of man and the world in Christ. The *mysterion* therefore
means both: the very content of faith, the knowledge of the divine
mystery revealed in Christ, and the saving power communicated
through and in the Church. As to the symbol, it is, within this
theology, the mode of the presence and action of the *mysterion*,
and primarily, although not exclusively, of its presence and action
in the liturgy, which is the privileged locus of the symbol. The

5. Bornert, *Les Commentaires*, p. 162. Cf. also N. Borgia, ed., *Il Commentario liturgico
   di S. Germano Patriarca Constantinopolitano e la versione latina de Anastasio
   Bibliotecaria,* Studi Liturgici 1, Grottaferrata, 1912.

symbol — and this is very important — is thus the very reality of that which it symbolizes. By representing, or signifying, that reality it makes it present, truly represents it. Nowhere is this symbolic realism more evident than in the application by Maximus of the term "symbol" to the Body and Blood of Christ offered in the Eucharist, an application which, in the context of today's opposition between the symbolic and the real, would be plain heresy.

It is only in the light of this theology of the *mysterion* and of the liturgy as its "mode" of presence and action that one can understand the liturgical symbolism proper to mystagogical commentaries. The liturgy, both in its totality and in each of its rites or actions, is symbol. The symbol, however, not of this or that particular event or person, but precisely of the whole *mysterion* as its revelation and saving grace. In other terms, this symbolism is not "illustrative" if by this word we mean the later symbolic identification of each liturgical act with one precise event of Christ's earthly life. Yes, the entrance, to use the example mentioned before, is the symbol of Christ's manifestation; but this liturgical manifestation refers to the entire mystery of His Incarnation and not merely to His appearance to the people after his baptism by John. And, in like manner, the entire liturgy is the symbol of the mystery of Christ's ascension and glorification, as well as of the mystery of the Kingdom of God, the "world to come." Through its symbols the liturgy gives us the *theoria:* the knowledge and the contemplation of these saving mysteries, just as, on another level of the same symbolism, the liturgy re-represents, makes present and active, the ascension of the human soul to God and communion with Him.

"Makes present." But it is precisely this function that the later illustrative symbolism, begins to lose, and precisely to the degree to which it becomes merely illustrative. When the celebrated Byzantine liturgical commentator, Symeon of Thessalonica,

writes that the seven items of the bishop's liturgical vestments
correspond to the seven actions of the Holy Spirit, that his mantle
symbolizes the "providential and almighty and all-preserving
grace of God," and then goes on explaining in the same manner
the whole liturgy, we know immediately that we are on a level of
symbolism radically different from the one proposed by Maximus
and the other mystagogical commentators. Different not only in
quality, as a masterpiece can differ from a less perfect painting
which nevertheless belongs to the same school and the same
tradition. Here the difference is precisely a discontinuity. And the
principle of that discontinuity is, as I said earlier, a theological
one. For Saint Maximus, the liturgical symbol is validated by a
consistent theology of the liturgy, which, in turn, applies to
liturgy a comprehensive and consistent theological vision. The
late Byzantine and post-Byzantine symbolism has ceased to belong to any theological context, to reflect any theology of the
liturgy. It has become, and remains even today, a self-centered
and self-contained "genre," identified, unfortunately, by many
with the very essence of the Byzantine liturgical tradition.

Having said all this, we still have not answered the most
important question: is there such an essence, is there a truly
adequate explanation of the Byzantine liturgical symbolism, and,
if so, where and how can we find it? For it must be clear, I am
sure, that for all its self-evident and indisputable superiority over
the later illustrative symbolism, the mystagogical symbolism of a
Saint Maximus cannot be simply equated with the Byzantine *lex
orandi*. Whatever its theological and spiritual consistency in itself,
it still is an interpretation superimposed on the liturgy whose
roots are in a theological theory rather than in the liturgical
evidence itself. It is certainly not an accident that the symbolic
interpretations of the liturgy belonging to this tradition — those
of Saint Gregory of Nyssa, of Pseudo-Dionysius, of Saint Maximus — are substantially different from one another, represent
different emphases, different varieties, although with the same

general, mystical, and mysteriological trend and orientation. The reason for this is that they apply to the liturgy their particular vision rather than seek in the liturgy the vision implied in its own *ordo*, in its own structures and texts, in short, in its own symbolism.

So the question is, is there such a vision, such a symbolism? To this question my answer is *"yes."* And the first formal and extrinsic proof of that "yes" is the remarkable resistance with which Byzantine worship as a whole, and, more specifically, the Eucharistic divine liturgy opposed, at least in the essential expressions of its form and spirit, the extremely powerful pressures of the various symbolic interpretations and reductions. There have been, to be sure, here and there something like "surrenders," some local "invasions" of the symbolism. On the whole however, the Byzantine liturgy has surprisingly well preserved its inner unity and the organic continuity of its centuries-long development.[6]

The term which, I submit, best expresses the initial liturgical experience of the Church, the experience which shaped and also maintained and preserved the fundamental *ordo* of Byzantine worship, is "eschatological symbolism." The word "eschatological," being used today in so many different meanings and connotations, requires that I explain my use of it in the general context of this paper. It refers first of all to the belief, central and overwhelming in the early Christian community, that the coming of Christ, His life, His death and resurrection from the dead, His ascension to heaven and the sending by Him, on the day of Pentecost, of the Holy Spirit, have brought about the Lord's Day; the *Yom Yahweh* announced by the prophets has inaugurated the new *aeon* of the Kingdom of God. Those who believe in Christ,

6. For details, cf. J. Mateos, *La célébration de la parole dans la liturgie byzantine*, Orientalia Christiana Analecta 191, Rome, 1971. And also J. Mateos, ed., *Le Typicon de la Grande Eglise*, Orientalia Christiana Analecta 165-166, Rome, 1962-1963.

while they still live in the old *aeon*, in what the New Testament calls "this world," already belong to the new *aeon;* for, united to Christ and anointed with the Holy Spirit, they have in them the new and eternal life and the power to overcome sin and death. The mode of the presence in this world of the "world to come," of the Kingdom of God, is the Church — the community of those united to Christ and in Him to one another. And the act by which the Church fulfills that presence, actualizes herself as the new people of God and the Body of Christ, is "the breaking of bread," the Eucharist by which she ascends to Christ's table in His Kingdom. This belief, which, I repeat, constitutes the very heart of the early Christian experience and faith, thus implies a tension; the tension between this world and the world to come, between being in this world, yet also and already not of this world. And it is this tension that constitutes, as I have tried to show in my book mentioned earlier, the basis, the formative principle of the early Christian worship and more especially of the acts central to it — of Baptism and Eucharist. They express and fulfill the Church as above all the passage, the *passover*, from the old into the new, from this world into the "day without evening" of Christ's Kingdom. In this world the Church is *in statu viae*, in pilgrimage and expectation, and her task is to preach the Gospel of the Kingdom, the "Good News" of salvation accomplished by Christ. But the Church can fulfill this task only because she herself already has access to the kingdom of whose joy and fullness she can thus be the witness to the ends of the world.

Only in the light of this eschatology can we understand the initial symbolism of the liturgy, the symbolism which I term "eschatological" and which, as I have said already, is both the starting point and also the principle of subsequent liturgical development. The essential character (I could say the particularity) of this eschatological symbolism, is not simply its realism in the sense of the presence in the sign of the reality which it signifies, for the same realism, as we have seen, is affirmed also by Saint

Maximus and the other representatives of the symbolism we termed "mysteriological." The essential particularity of the eschatological symbolism is the fact that in it the very distinction between the sign and the signified is simply ignored. For Saint Maximus and even more for the later mysteriological symbolism, this distinction between sign and signified is essential, because in their view the liturgical act which we perform today reveals, communicates, or simply represents an act performed in the past, the present, or the future by somebody else — Christ, the apostles, the angels. Thus, in this perspective, during the liturgical rite of entrance it is we who enter, but this entrance symbolizes the appearance of Christ. The sign is distinct from the reality it reveals or represents. But this is exactly the opposite of what is actually occurring in the liturgical signs. The whole point of the eschatological symbolism is that in it the sign and that which it signifies are one and the same thing. The liturgy, we may say, happens to *us*. The liturgical entrance is our, or rather, the Church's entrance to heaven. We do not symbolize the presence of the angels; we *do*, however, join them in their unceasing glorification of God. Our offering to God of the gifts of bread and wine is our sacrifice of ourselves; the entire liturgy is the Church's ascension to Christ's table in His kingdom, just as the Eucharistic gifts sanctified by the Holy Spirit are the Body and Blood of Christ. And we do all this and we are all this because we are *in Christ*, because the Church herself is our entrance, our passage into the new *aeon* bestowed upon us by Christ's incarnation, death, resurrection, and ascension.

Lack of time prevents me from showing that it is this eschatological experience of the Church that shaped and determined the entire development of the Christian liturgy, and not only of the sacraments but also of the liturgical cycles of time, i.e., the year, the week, and the day. Even today, after an extremely complex development over many centuries, the Byzantine *Typikon* remains ultimately incomprehensible unless we discern in it, as the key to its complex rules, prescriptions, and rubrics, the eschatological experience of the early Church: the experience, for example, of Sunday as the eighth day, the day beyond the seven days of creation and therefore beyond the fallen world, the day of the new creation of which we partake in the Eucharistic ascension; the experience of Pascha, later extended to other feasts, as the passage, the pass-over into the joy of the Kingdom of God; the experience, in fact, of the whole worship, to use a favorite Byzantine formula, as heaven on earth.

But, and this is the main point of all that I wanted to say, it is this eschatological symbolism that remains, in spite of all theological, mystical, and illustrative interpretations and explanations, the essential symbolism of the Byzantine liturgy. When, having read all the innumerable commentaries, we return from the "rich symbolism" which they find in Byzantine worship to the liturgy itself, to the testimony of its prayers and rites, of its *ordo* and rhythm, we experience a kind of spiritual liberation. For what we discover then is the genuine liturgical theology, and this means the theology for which liturgy is not a "object," but its very source. We discover, in other terms, the forgotten truth of the ancient saying: *lex orandi est lex credendi.*

9

Sacrifice and Worship

There are many aspects of the idea of sacrifice, but I would like to begin with my chief interest, which is worship.[1] This seems to me to be the very center of the whole idea of sacrifice, and the place where all its facets come together: renunciation, offering up and transformation.

There was a controversy which developed in the West about the Eucharist as sacrifice. On the one hand, there was the concept that by accepting the sacrifice of Christ as unique and full, the sacrificial aspect of the Eucharist must be rejected; and on the other hand, there was the scholastic idea, which defined sacrifice only in terms of redemption and atonement — something bloody which satisfies divine anger or justice. I always felt the whole debate wrong, for that kind of theology and that kind of religion interpret sacrifice as a legal transaction: a satisfaction is required, a duty of the creation to the Creator, like an income tax: the oblation of the best animal or even of the child, to satisfy an objective necessity. This is the perspective which I think needs not only correction but a much more radical rethinking, starting with the very nature of sacrifice, which has been forgotten by the theologians and sometimes rediscovered in the study of religions.

I would like to point out that first of all, sacrifice is an ontology. It is not just a result of something, it is a major expression or a first revelation of life itself; it is life's spiritual content. Where there is no sacrifice there is no life. Sacrifice is rooted in the recognition of life as love: as giving up, not because I want more

1. First published in *Parabola*, 3/2, 1978, pp. 60-65.

for myself, or to satisfy an objective justice, but because it is the only way of reaching the fullness that is possible for me.

So before sacrifice becomes expiation, reparation, or redemption, it is life's own natural movement. All this I find in the eastern Eucharist, where before we come to the crucifixion, we speak of the sacrifice of praise, and of salvation as a return to the sacrificial way of life. Opposed to sacrifice is consumerism: the idea that everything belongs to me and I have to grab it — and we are restored from that only by the complex movement exemplified by the Eucharist where we offer ourselves and are accepted through Christ's offering of Himself.

So, contrary to some scholars and phenomenologists of religion, I would say that the origin of the sacrifice is not so much *fear* as the need for communion in the real sense: a communion as giving and sharing. One part of the animal which we eat is burned and offered up to God, which means that we are sharing food with God and so become consubstantial with him. I think this is much more the primitive idea of sacrifice than any other idea. The authority of the sacrifice is in giving, because giving *is* life; it is a giving-and-receiving, and therefore this whole movement is central and reciprocal.

So much of the western theological viewpoint has either fear behind it or else some kind of easy over-optimism; and that is a different spiritual climate for us within Eastern Orthodoxy. It is very difficult to express the experience of the Eastern Church in these terms. Take the whole tradition of the sacrifice of the Mass: the broken body, the shed blood. We in Eastern Orthodoxy see the bread and wine as symbolizing creation; the wine is a eucharistic gift not because it looks like blood, but because blood is life, and wine is something which makes the heart of man glad. Therefore when we raise to God the Offertory at the beginning of the Eucharistic observance, we haven't yet reached the Cross and the Passion, we are simply and joyfully restored to that situation in which we come to partake of life; the bread and wine is what is to become *my* body and *my* blood. This is the fundamental thing. The happiness is because in Christ we have access to that sacrificial life. We not only give up but go up; there is no end to the possibility of going up.

It is not that there is no evil, as some people would have us think, including, I am afraid, Teilhard de Chardin; that is the weakness I find in him. Evil is very important and sacrifice has something to do with that; but we have to establish the perspective in which the idea of sacrifice would not be reduced only to that of expiation and atonement for sin. We have to get rid of that narrow view, and on the other hand we have to get rid of an over-optimism that says all we have to do now is make every action a joyful offering. No, in this world Christ is crucified, as Pascal says; evil is a real presence, and the sacrificial idea is that most certainly joy cannot be reached without suffering; but suffering as exemplified in the Crucifixion is in itself a victory. The meaning of Christ's death is not that death is satisfied; it is a changing of the signs. But death is still death. We explain that by the doctrine of Christ's descent into Hades.

The whole perspective of sacrifice depends on the starting point. The beginning is before there is any sin or evil, with something that belongs to the real life. Then comes the second stage: evil, betrayal, suffering, death. Sacrifice remains there, but it acquires a new energy, and goes on finally to the third stage, the eschatological meaning: the end of all things, the fulfillment of all things in the perfect sacrifice, the perfect communion, the perfect unity. These are the three dimensions of sacrifice which it seems to me have to be restored for a balanced view and theology of sacrifice. I think that all these aspects are essential: thanksgiving, communion, giving up, sharing, transformation. They are all necessary to give this fuller view.

In the idea of communion, the question arises as to what is

man's part; how does he fill his sacrificial role? Perhaps God also needs to be fed; and here, it seems to me, we could think of the place of food in the story of the creation and the fall. In the mythology of creation, man is created a hungry being; that is why God made the world as his food. Man is dependent; and dependence is an objective slavery. But if God is the master and we are just slaves, what can He receive from a universe where everything depends on Him? This is where sacrifice enters, and priesthood. The priest is first and foremost the sacrificer — I am not speaking now of priesthood in the church's terms — and so he is the man who can freely transform that dependence: he is the man who can say *thank you*. For the moment when the slave whom God has created can thank Him for his life and for his food, he is liberated; sacrifice, the thank-offering, is liberating. I have always understood the fall (or what is called "original sin") as the loss of man's desire to be a priest; or perhaps you might say the desire he has *not* to be a priest but a consumer, and then little by little he begins to consider that to eat and to live are his rights, which is a total enslavement, because there is no end to "rights." Dostoevsky in *The Possessed* shows us the man who wants his final right, to be God; so he commits suicide, to prove that he is free, like God. But it is the offering, the thanksgiving and the praise that make us truly free. The mystery of the food is that it has no meaning unless it becomes life. The food I eat is dead, and its resurrection in me must be something more than calories and proteins; it must be truly the sacrament of sacrifice.

Perhaps we should touch on that extreme aspect of sacrifice which is martyrdom, which I think should be differentiated from heroism. We find the latter almost everywhere, even among animals. It is a very respectable virtue, of course, and I don't mean to denigrate it, but martyrdom is altogether different. The martyrs were witnesses: witnesses of the transformation of death. What Christ destroys is not physical death but spiritual death, which is the alienation we live in — alienation from one another, from the world, from nature, from God, from ourselves first of all. The first Christian martyr, Stephen, as he was dying, said: "I see heaven opening." He witnessed death becoming life. The "birthdays" of the martyrs are celebrated by the Church on their death days, on that day they were "born." The martyr does not think of this death as an increase in the capital of good deeds on which the Church can later draw checks, but as a sacrifice of love and praise; he is given the fantastic privilege of joining Christ in the death which is not an accident, but the culmination of a life filled to the brim.

But we don't have to go as far as martyrdom to find the real function of suffering. We all suffer, usually very passively; but there is another kind of suffering which I impose on myself when I "sacrifice" or "give up" something. This is the suffering of someone who returns from a fall. There was a Russian poet who said, "Give me, O Lord, the strength to face Thy *austere* Paradise." He used the word "austere"; this is different from the usual devotion to the pleasure principle, the notion that in the life eternal everything will be easy. The idea is rather that suffering is the very means of return, of discovery and of growth. That is the idea in Teilhard de Chardin, that it is the condition for growing; everything that grows, suffers. So there is a suffering which is chosen because there is no other way of reaching my real self. It is not that God has created suffering, I have created it myself by falling away from that life; and to return to it is painful. It requires a discipline.

That raises the whole question of today's approach to life, and to medicine. Of course there is a glorious growth of medical knowledge; on the other hand, I am afraid we are coming soon to a society in which suffering will be simply forbidden, by law. That is not a joke; it is very terrible. Already in church it is very difficult to preach anything that disturbs people; one must always preach some kind of happy ending to everything. I think the religious reaction should be a restoration of the real meaning of suffering, and I see that people, because they cannot face suffering any more, are falling into mental disease. The whole idea of the welfare state tends toward the belief that suffering is a crime against nature; you must not suffer.

Now I do not believe that God made suffering and death; He didn't create a world in which every love ends in separation, in which everything is exactly the opposite of what we wish; and to understand this, the liturgy is always taking us back to that moment when God, having created the world, "saw that it was very good." It is only when something very good is broken that you will pay almost any price to restore it. This is our participation: the sacrifice is not for out profit alone. It adds to that energy in the world which recreates life. Christ, using a massive weapon, makes death a servant of life, by making His death a sacrifice, by giving it with love. He makes even death into life. And it is of this that the martyrs are the witnesses, and the participants.

There is a great depth of meaning in sacrifice, and a synthesis of its aspects which have broken down in our time needs to be remade. Maybe there is truth in almost every theory, if one brings them all together and starts with sacrifice as the very content of God-created life, because God Himself is sacrificial, a constant giving, a sharing with His creation; and ultimately what He needs in return, what will "feed" Him, is love.

It is strange that our concepts of sacrifice should be so poor, for the real meaning is in the very name: to make whole, or holy — it is the same word. The breaking down of that meaning is the essence of secularism and consumerism. Secularism is not, as some people think, the denial of God; that kind of religion which offers health and therapy of all kinds is compatible with secularism: the idea that you need a pharmacy, you need a psychotherapist, and you need religion in order to be healthy. I have never considered the secular view simply atheistic, but a denial of the sacrifice: of the holy and the whole, of the priesthood as a way of life. The secular idea is that everybody needs religion because it helps to keep law and order, comforts us, and so on; it is that point of view which denies levels. But the whole terminology of the early Church is of ascension to another level: "He ascended into Heaven." Since He is man, we ascend in Him. Christianity begins to fall down as soon as the idea of our going up in Christ's ascension — the movement of sacrifice — begins to be replaced by His going down. And this is exactly where we are today: it is always a bringing Him down into ordinary life, and this we say will solve our social problems. The Church must go down to the ghettos, into the world in all its reality. But to save the world from social injustices, the need first of all is not so much to go down to its miseries, as to have a few witnesses in this world to the possible ascension.

10

Liturgical Theology: Remarks on Method

Translated from the French by Thomas Fisch

I

The liturgical movement, whose "golden age" occurred from 1920 to 1950, conferred upon the study of the liturgy (liturgical studies) a theological status which it had never commanded previously within the system of the sacred sciences, as this system developed and crystallized after the end of the Patristic age, first in the West and then — under western influence — in the East.[1] If there did exist within this system a certain theology of the liturgy (reduced, to be sure, almost solely to a theology of the sacraments), the very possibility of liturgical theology itself was excluded. It is the "discovery" of this distinction between theology of the liturgy and liturgical theology which stands, in my opinion, as the principal attainment of the liturgical movement. All methodological reflection on the relations between theology (the *lex credendi*) on the one hand and the liturgy (the *lex orandi*) on the other must begin from this fundamental distinction.

I designate by "theology of the liturgy" all study of the Church's cult in which this cult is analyzed, understood and defined in its "essence" as well as in its "forms" with the help of

---

1. Résumé of the communication which I was to have presented at the 28th Conférence Saint-Serge in June, 1981. Unfortunately I was not able to take part in the conference nor to compose a complete version of my communication. I am confined to submitting only this "draft" while apologizing to my confrères. A.S. Originally published in *La liturgie; son sens, son esprit, sa méthode.* Conférences Saint-Serge, XXVIII Semaine d'Études Liturgiques, Paris, June 30 through July 3, 1981 (B.E.L. Subsidia vol. 27), Roma, Edizioni liturgiche, 1982, pp. 297–303.

and in terms of theological categories and concepts which are exterior to the cult itself, that is, to its liturgical *specificity*. In this case, in other words, the liturgy is "subordinated" to, if not subject to, theology because it receives from theology its "meaning" as well as the definition of its place and function within the church. Thus, here it is theology alone which determines (and, even more, determines *a priori*) what within the liturgy constitutes a *locus theologicus*, as well as what is of use theologically and what is not, and it is thus theology alone which assigns to the liturgy its theological value or "coefficient."

It is to this state of affairs (is it necessary to remind anyone?) that the liturgy has fallen since the appearance of that theology known as "systematic," which sets itself over against the idea of *liturgical theology*. Liturgical theology, on the other hand, is based upon the recognition that the liturgy in its totality is not only an "object" of theology, but above all its *source*, and this by virtue of the liturgy's essential ecclesial function: i.e., that of revealing by the means which are proper to it (and which belong only to it) the faith of the church; in other words, of being that *lex orandi* in which the *lex credendi* finds its principal criterion and standard.

Once the above distinction is articulated, it is evident that this liturgical theology, whose necessity and also whose possibility were revealed by the liturgical movement, has not been, until now, the object of any methodological reflection. The liturgical movement, though it was an event and movement of primary importance, did not result in any "seizure" of doctrinal or theological consciousness. This fact is the probable cause of that strange defeat which followed so closely upon the movement's "triumph." The liturgical movement's victory very quickly yielded to an immense confusion, a veritable liturgical crisis whose end, let us speak frankly, is not yet in sight.

The crisis broke out and is particularly visible in the West. But let us not delude ourselves; it has already fully exceeded its specifically western context and is about to appear for the Orthodox Church as well, although in quite a different way and in a contrasting "tonality."

This crisis is chiefly the result of a profound misinterpretation of the liturgical awakening, a misinterpretation which has become manifest everywhere since the beginning of this century. It is above all a misinterpretation of the liturgical awakening's "reformist" orientation. Given the profusion and depth of the movement's "discoveries," it was inevitable that this awakening should pose the question of *liturgical reform*. But if, in the view of that movement and its animators, such a reform was conceived first of all as a *return* to the genuine liturgical tradition after many centuries of impoverishment and decadence, that very perspective was ignored by the *aggiornamento* generation, completely drowned as it was in its reformist zeal. In this situation the idea of liturgical reform acquired a radically different meaning from that which it had within the liturgical movement. In the context of such *aggiornamento*, the liturgy itself became a privileged place to carry out the struggle for the integration of the Church with the modern world and with its problems and aspirations. From this a type of confusion, even chaos, followed, which is all the more dangerous in that this secularizing reform very often appropriated to itself the terminology and vocabulary proper to the liturgical movement.

The predictable and inevitable result of such confusion was the violent reaction of a conservatism and a fundamentalism equally opposed to all liturgical reform. One can say without any exaggeration that, liberated by the liturgical movement from the former scholastic and legalist tyranny, the liturgy now finds itself dominated once again by various ideologies which remain deluded about its true nature and its essential function in the church.

It is from this fact that the urgent necessity arises of coming back again to the work which the liturgical movement and its

moving spirits could not or perhaps dared not undertake, that of
a reflection upon the very object of liturgical theology itself and
on the method which springs from it. I repeat, the liturgical
movement was above all an *event*. It produced some admirable
works. But the confusion which smothered it at the very moment
when it seemed to "triumph" is the best evidence that it has not
yet been understood and "digested" by the church, due to the lack
of reflection on its theological meaning.

II

Our first question, therefore, is this: "What is the object of
liturgical theology insofar as it is *theology?*" I stress the latter word
because, to the degree that it is a historical discipline, liturgical
studies has been accepted for a long time within the family of the
sacred sciences, where it occupies a modest but well-defined place.
As Dom Fernand Cabrol states in his chapter of *Origines liturgiques* devoted to the liturgy as science, "If history is a science, it is
possible for liturgical studies to be a science under the same claim
as epigraphy, numismatics, paleography, diplomacy and all the
philological sciences which are auxiliaries to history and are subject to its laws."[2] No theological pretension here. The "scientific"
study of the liturgy is a historical discipline and, according to
Dom Cabrol, one which is so developed that "the work which
remains to be done is neither the most interesting nor the easi-
est."[3] We find more theological interest shown towards the
branch of liturgical studies devoted to the *euchological* and *hymno-
graphic* study of the liturgy, of the texts of which the liturgy is
composed. Although these investigations are important and useful, no such study can be identified simply with liturgical theology. For example, the Byzantine liturgy has been and remains
literally inundated with hymnography and, as we all know, often

2. Dom F. Cabrol, *Origines Liturgiques*, Paris, 1907, p. 25.
3. *Idem, Introduction aux études liturgiques*, Paris, 1907, p. 39.

this is to the detriment of other essential elements of the liturgical celebration, in particular of its biblical dimension. But next to some admirable successes of great theological value, one also finds in this material certain texts and suites of hymnography whose rhetorical and artificial character obscures more than reveals the true sense of particular celebrations.

On the other hand, if the *word* and thus the texts are, by all evidence, the essential expression of the Christian cult (the very medium of the liturgical *epiphany*), they also form the most *variable* part of the liturgical tradition. Even within one "liturgical family" there can be great differences on the level of terminology and liturgical language. The two eucharistic anaphoras of the Byzantine liturgy, those of St John Chrysostom and of St Basil, provide a good example. The difference between the former's concise wording and the opulent theological formulations of the latter is impressive. Is this to say that, because it is longer and richer in doctrinal content, the anaphora of St Basil is "better"? Certainly it is better as a magisterial résumé of the church's trinitarian faith (and that is why, I think, it is prescribed for catechetical and baptismal seasons like Lent). But it is by no means "better" if one applies the liturgical test, in other words if one regards it as a eucharistic anaphora whose essential function is not to explain but precisely to manifest, to be an epiphany of the mysteries of faith.

What makes the unity of the anaphora, therefore, is not its verbal expressions, which have varied greatly in time and space, but above all its structure, that "shape" or "form" of which Dom Gregory Dix has spoken so well. It is within this "shape" that the words — which have varied a great deal from one region to another — acquire their full meaning and accomplish their liturgical function.

III

These observations bring us back to our question concerning the object of liturgical theology. We have seen that for Dom Cabrol's generation liturgical study, reduced to history, was essentially an auxiliary science, lacking any links to the theology which itself "governs" the liturgy without bothering to be preoccupied with history. Nevertheless it is this "historical school" which, probably without realizing it, prepared the advent of the liturgical movement and thus of the liturgical theology to which that movement could not fail to lead. For, in effect, it was the *historical* rediscovery of the liturgy (accomplished, so to speak, outside of the official theology) which made possible the liturgy's *theological* rediscovery. In truth, it is the historians of the liturgy who, without attempting to do so, have helped us to discover this *specificity* of the liturgy which makes it the source of a *sui generis* theology, a theology of which the liturgy is both the unique source and the unique revelation.

This specificity, let us immediately note, consists in the *eschatological* character of the Christian cult whose essential "function" is to *realize* the church by revealing her as the epiphany of the Kingdom of God. In this sense the Christian cult is unique, without analogies and without antecedents within the universal phenomenon of religious cult and especially in comparison with the mystery cults to which some people so frequently want to reduce it. For this "uniqueness" of the Christian cult comes to it exclusively from the Christian faith which, if it is on the one hand a belief comparable to all other beliefs, is on the other hand the possession and the experience of the object of this belief: the Kingdom of God itself. This Kingdom, which for "this world" is *yet to come* and forms the ultimate horizon of its history, is already present (revealed, communicated, given, accepted...) in the Church. And it is the liturgy which accomplishes this presence and this *parousia*, and which in this sense (in its totality) is the *sacrament of the church* and thus the *sacrament of the Kingdom.* Whether it be the sacraments, or the liturgical year — from Pascha to Pascha — or the week lived in remembrance of and in waiting for the Eighth Day, the Day of the Lord; it is always this eschatological reality, this foretaste, this anticipation of the Kingdom of God which is offered to us by the liturgy. But it is the Eucharist which, by all evidence, constitutes the heart and center of this eschatological *experience.* In it and through it the Church realizes herself in her ascension to the table of the Lord in his Kingdom in order that she might have the power to bear witness to that Kingdom in "this world." As the Fathers said, the Eucharist is the "sacrament of sacraments."

Of *this* experience the liturgy is the sole and unique source and realization. And that is why it is the only genuine source of the church's *comprehending* of her own nature and eschatological vocation or, more simply, of the Christian eschatology. It is possible to say that liturgical theology has as its proper domain or "object" eschatology itself, which is revealed in its fullness through the liturgy. And if today it is necessary for us to "rediscover" all of this, that is because the essential tragedy within the history of the church has been the nearly total eclipse of the eschatological "content" and inspiration which are so evident in the faith and life of the primitive church. But in that case everything has been warped: eschatological doctrine, but sacramental doctrine as well, and ecclesiology ... but also liturgical piety. Eschatology was relegated to the end of the theological manuals into a chapter *De Novissimis* which was exclusively personal and futurist. The sacraments were defined and understood as so many means of personal sanctification. Ecclesiology was reduced to a total institutionalism, and piety to an individualism complete in and closed upon itself. It is accordingly high time that the experience of the liturgical movement, although regrettably short-lived, be translated and consolidated into a liturgical theology which alone today can restore to us that unique eschatological energy and perspective which makes us the people of God, acquainted with the true sense of the ancient formula: "*in* this world but not *of this world* ..."

IV

If the *object* of liturgical theology which I have attempted to describe and define in an obviously very general and even superficial manner is thus acknowledged, the method poses no real problems. It consists of three steps:

1) In the first step the question is to establish *the liturgical fact.* This is clearly a matter for liturgical history, which has made enormous progress since the time of Cabrol and other historians of the Christian cult, especially in the areas of *comparative history* of the liturgy and of *phenomenology of religion.*

2) The second step is that of *theological analysis* of this liturgical fact. Whether it concerns a feast or a sacramental rite, a text or a celebration, the theological "content" or "coefficient" of each of theses liturgical components requires that each be situated in the theological context which is proper to it in order to be understood and defined. To take only one example, the interminable controversy over the eucharistic *epiclesis* has never escaped from the impasse in which it existed from the beginning, because both sides — the West and the East — have continued to impose on the problem theological categories and, in general, a problematic profoundly alien to the liturgy itself.

3) The third and, obviously, the most important step is that of synthesis, the release of the inherent theological meaning from the witness of the liturgical *epiphany* itself.

It is plain that each of these steps should be the object of a thorough study. In these notes, which are, alas, only some *membra disiecta*, I have limited myself to a general sketch. For if we know what we expect from liturgical theology, that very theology is what remains to be done.

Postscript

A Life Worth Living

John Meyendorff

The thoughts and feelings expressed by those who had the opportunity to speak at Fr Alexander Schmemann's funeral services — hierarchs, colleagues and friends — reflect all that needs to be said in these first weeks after his untimely death on December 13, 1983.[1] Others perhaps will eventually undertake a more thorough evaluation of his thought and writings, including that which remains unpublished. My task here is only to point to the main periods of his life, without pretending to be exhaustive. As one writes about a very close friend — almost a brother — it is, however, impossible to be totally objective, to avoid being somewhat subjective and impressionistic in interpreting what was truly significant in Fr Alexander's life — a life truly worth living! For this subjectivity I apologize in advance.

Born in 1921 into a Russian family, with Baltic German ancestors on his father's side, Fr Alexander moved to France from Estonia in his early childhood. The life of the Russian emigration in Paris became his life until his departure for America in 1951.

The "Russian Paris" of the 1930s was a world unto itself. Numbering tens of thousands and including intellectuals, artists, theologians, grand dukes and former tsarist ministers, publishing daily papers and settling political divisions in hot arguments, Russian émigrés still dreamt of a return home. Children were reared in Russian schools, somewhat in isolation from the sur-

1. First published in *St Vladimir's Theological Quarterly*, 28, 1984, pp. 3-10.

rounding French society (which actually was not always very hospitable to them). The young Alexander (or Sasha, as he was called by family and friends) tasted something of that secluded Russian education: he spent several years as a "cadet," in a Russian military school in Versailles, and then transferred to a *gimnaziia* (high school). Whatever the merits of that initial schooling, it hardly satisfied his mind and aspirations. Even then he felt that the best in the great legacy of Russian culture (particularly Russian literature) was not closed to the West, but was, on the contrary, necessarily "European" in scope. Dostoevsky's famous "Pushkin speech" represented for him the only valid understanding of Russia and of Russian civilization. He refused to accept its artificial limitation, and pursued studies at a French lycée and the University of Paris.

Already as a teenager, Alexander discovered his true spiritual home in the Church. His initiation to Orthodoxy and its authentic spirit took place not so much at the dull, compulsory religion classes given at the military school or the *gimnaziia*, but rather through active participation in the liturgy at the monumental St Alexander Nevsky Cathedral on *rue Daru*, as an altar boy and later as a sub-deacon. Inspired by the eminently wise and always gracious personality of Metropolitan Evlogy, by a clergy a little "old régime" but also enlightened and open, by the dedicated leadership of Dr Peter Kovalevsky (who headed the large staff of "minor" clergy at the cathedral), Alexander understood the value and dimensions of the liturgy and even developed a certain love for pomp and ceremony, which remained with him all his life.

The years of World War II and the German occupation of France were years of decisive options. Providentially sheltered from the tragedies of war, Alexander studied at the Theological Institute of Paris (1940-1945) and married Juliana Ossorguine (1943), then a student in classics at the Sorbonne and a member of a traditional, church-oriented Russian family. It became quite clear in those years, to all his friends and acquaintances, that Alexander had found his true vocation, and also that God had blessed him with successful marriage and family life. The inspiration and joy that he found then contributed much to the power with which, in all later years, he was able to communicate their content to others.

The Orthodox Theological Institute in Paris — "St Sergius," as it is frequently called — had gathered a somewhat heterogeneous but remarkable faculty, which included representatives of the old theological establishment of prerevolutionary Russia (A V Kartashev), intellectuals who came to Orthodoxy during the revolution (V V Zenkovsky) and former students at Belgrade (Fr Cyprian Kern, Fr N Afanassiev). The school was still dominated by the personality of Fr Sergius Bulgakov, a former Russian seminarian, then a Marxist philosopher and finally — through the influence of Vladimir Soloviev and Paul Florensky — a priest and a theologian. During the war years at St Sergius the students were few, but the enthusiasm and the hopes for an Orthodox revival remained strong.

Never attracted by the "sophiological" speculations of Bulgakov — for whom, however, he had the greatest personal respect — Alexander Schmemann was primarily seeking specialization in church history. He became a pupil of A V Kartashev, whose brilliant lectures and skeptical mind matched Schmemann's own tendency to critical analysis of reality around him. The result was a "candidate's thesis" (equivalent to an MDiv) on Byzantine theocracy. Having completed the five-year program of studies at St Sergius, Schmemann became an instructor in church history, first as a layman, then as a priest, following his ordination by the then Archbishop Vladimir (Tikhonitsky) in 1946, who was heading the Russian Exarchate of Western Europe under the jurisdiction of the Patriarchate of Constantinople.

Besides A V Kartashev, two other members of the St Sergius

faculty exercised a decisive influence upon Fr Schmemann. Archimandrite Cyprian (Kern), his spiritual father and friend, also took him as his assistant in the SS Constantine and Helen parish in Clamart, near Paris. Fr Cyprian taught patristics at St Sergius, but his love was for the liturgy and his liturgical taste had a lasting influence on Fr Schmemann. Both also shared knowledge and appreciation of Russian classical literature. Intellectually more decisive, however, was Fr Schmemann's acquaintance with and devotion to the ecclesiological ideas of Fr Nicholas Afanassiev, a professor of canon law whose name will be forever attached to what he called "eucharistic ecclesiology" and whose ideas are reflected in many of Fr Schmemann's writings.

As a young instructor in Church History, Fr Schmemann planned to write a doctoral dissertation on the Council of Florence. He eventually abandoned that topic, but the publication of a short treatise by St Mark of Ephesus on "The Resurrection" remains from that initial interest in Byzantine studies. Actually, the Church itself always stood at the center of Fr Alexander's spiritual and intellectual interests and commitments. His discussion of Byzantine theocracy, and his readings in Church History in general — as well as his initial dissertation topic — came from his concern with the *survival* of the Church, as Church, during the centuries of an ambiguous alliance with the State, and the survival of Orthodoxy in its medieval confrontation with Rome. But, perhaps, he lacked the necessary patience for remaining concentrated on the Church's past: the existential *today* was that which really mattered. And *today*, the Orthodox Church could not be alive either as a defense of the State, or cultural appendix of "Russianism": it was alive in and through the Liturgy. Here, the ecclesiology of Afanassiev provided the direction (although not really the model) for Fr Alexander's further orientation as a theologian.

It is quite clear that Fr Alexander's theological worldview was shaped during his Paris years. But, although the influence of some of his teachers at St Sergius was decisive, he always lived in a wider spiritual world. The forties and fifties were a period of extraordinary theological revival in French Roman Catholicism — the years of a "return to the sources" and a "liturgical movement." It is from that existing milieu that Fr Schmemann really learned "liturgical theology," a "philosophy of time" and the true meaning of the "paschal mystery." The names and ideas of Jean Daniélou, Louis Bouyer, and several others are inseparable from the shaping of Fr Schmemann's mind. And if their legacy was somewhat lost within the turmoil of postconciliar Roman Catholicism, their ideas produced much fruit in the organically-liturgical and ecclesiologically-consistent world of Orthodoxy through the brilliant and always effective witness of Fr Schmemann.

Orthodoxy in France was not made up only of intellectual or theological pursuits. The breakdown of all reasonable hopes for a swift return to Russia raised the immediate issue of a permanent survival of Orthodoxy in the West and involved the question: Why did an Orthodox "diaspora" occur at all? Together with most representatives of the "younger" generation of Orthodox theologians, Fr Schmemann saw no other answer and no other meaning for the existence of the "diaspora" than the establishment of a territorial, eventually French-speaking local Church in France. His opposition to a return to the jurisdiction of the Moscow patriarchate was primarily based on the hope that the ecumenical patriarchate, under whose protection the Russian "exarchate" of western Europe had placed itself in 1931, would initiate and sponsor such a gradual Orthodox unification according to canonical norms. Most Russians, however — including the older generation of St Sergius professors — rather saw the Constantinopolitan allegiance negatively, as a shield against Moscow's control — not as an opportunity for a mission to the West. Here lies one of the important elements which eventually encouraged Fr Alexander and his family to look to America for better conditions of realizing a more consistent Orthodox ecclesiology in the concrete life of the Church.

The decisive factor, which determined the departure of Fr Alexander for the United States, was the return to Paris from Eastern Europe of Fr Georges Florovsky, and his eventual appointment as Dean of St Vladimir's Seminary in New York.

Fr Florovsky had taught at St Sergius before the war, but his relationships with his colleagues were not easy. This uneasiness was partly due to his criticism of the sophiology of Fr Bulgakov (a criticism which, however, appears only indirectly in his writings). Rescued from Soviet-occupied Czechoslovakia in 1947, through the mediation of ecumenical friends, Fr Florovsky could not resume his chair of Patristics at St Sergius (it was now occupied by Fr Cyprian Kern). He taught Moral Theology for a short while and then accepted the post at St Vladimir's in New York (1949). Fr Schmemann became fascinated by the brightness of Florovsky's theological mind, by his vision of the Orthodox mission to the West, by his criticism of accepted nationalistic stereotypes, by the fact that he succeeded in being both rooted in the Church's past and fully open to the best theological movements of Western Christendom.

The fact that Fr Schmemann left for America (1951) and joined the faculty of St Vladimir's then being built up by Fr Florovsky, was felt at St Sergius as something of a betrayal, especially since it was eventually followed by similar moves by S S Verhovskoy (1953), and, later, by John Meyendorff (1959). The subsequent history and development of Orthodoxy in America does appear to show that the moves were justified, especially since St Sergius itself, although deprived of some of its faculty, not only survived, but eventually turned its programs and orientation in the pan-Orthodox direction, which made survival possible.

The early fifties were not easy years for St Vladimir's Seminary, then located in the extremely modest quarters of Reed House, on

Broadway and 121st Street. Conflicts of temperament and style are at the bottom of the regrettable resignation of Fr Florovsky (1955), who by the mere prestige of his personality had placed St Vladimir's on the academic and theological map of the country. Only in 1962, when the Seminary acquired its present campus in Crestwood, N.Y., did Fr Alexander assume the post of Dean, which he held until his death in 1983.

It is probably too early to speak in details of the last and longest period of his life in America, associated with the Seminary and with the Church at large. Perhaps the single most obvious contribution of Fr Alexander to the life of St Vladimir's was that he succeeded in integrating the school within the very texture of ecclesiastical life. During his tenure, it ceased to be simply an academic institution, respected in ecumenical circles, but rather heterogeneous to the life of dioceses and parishes. St Vladimir's produced priests, and these priests, serving not only within the "Russian Metropolia," but also in other jurisdictions (particularly the Antiochian and the Serbian) were taught the spirit of a universal and missionary Orthodox Church, transcending purely ethnic concerns. Also, St Vladimir's became the center of a liturgical and eucharistic revival, which is recognized and praised by both Metropolitan Theodosius and Metropolitan Philip in their homilies at the time of Fr Alexander's death. Fully committed to his work in America, Fr Schmemann did not break links with Europe. It is there at his *alma mater* of St Sergius that he obtained his doctorate in 1959, with Fr Nicholas Afanassiev and the present writer acting as examiners.

A real watershed in Fr Alexander's career in America was the establishment of the autocephalous Orthodox Church in America in 1970. If there was any commitment which was constant in his life, already in France, it was the hope that the uncanonical overlapping of "jurisdictions," which was the single most obvious obstacle to Orthodox witness in the West, would be replaced by local Church unity in conformity not only with the canons, but with the most essential requirements of Orthodox ecclesiology. Fr Alexander — and those of us who were committed in the same fundamental aspirations — hoped that the ecumenical patriarchate of Constantinople would contribute to (and possibly lead) Orthodox unity in America, for example through the "Standing Conference of Orthodox Bishops." But a role for Constantinople in such a process of unification would have required the consent of all other Orthodox Churches, including the Patriarchate of Moscow, whose jurisdiction in America was never denied by the Metropolia and was always sustained by American civil courts. On the other hand, Constantinople, very demanding in theory, was in practice quite inconsistent (it terminated its jurisdiction over the Russian diocese of France and called it to return to the Patriarchate of Moscow in 1965). The other churches would clearly not even envisage transferring their "diasporas" to the Greek patriarch. Realistically, the basis for Orthodoxy unity was rather to be found in the policies which the Russian Church always followed in principle, since it first established Orthodoxy in North America. Its canonical and missionary aim had always been a Church for Americans, established with the blessing of the Mother Churches and inviting all those who were interested freely to join in. This last offer implied, of course, that unity could not be established unilaterally, that the free consent of all was required. Of course, the Patriarchate of Constantinople was still welcome to assume leadership in an eventual unification process.

During the negotiations leading to autocephaly, a remarkable personal link was established between Fr Alexander and Metropolitan Nikodim (Rotov) of Leningrad, whose full understanding of the historical opportunity for Orthodoxy in America and singlehanded effectiveness in realizing the common goal made possible the signing of the Tomos of Autocephaly, on April 10, 1970, by Patriarch Alexis of Moscow. This act, however, was understood both by the Mother Church of Russia and its daughter-church in America, as the first — and not the last — step towards Orthodox unity to be realized through conciliar assent of all Orthodox Churches.

In the midst of his work as teacher and his involvement in the life of the Church — with lectures, articles, addresses and meetings all over the country — Fr Schmemann never lost another concern which he held since his youth: the fate of Orthodoxy in Russia. The opportunity he had for years to address a weekly sermon in Russian on "Radio Liberty" made his name known to many among the ghettoized and repressed Christians in Russia. One of them was Alexander Solzhenitzyn, whose writings, smuggled abroad, were for Fr Alexander — as for many others — a breath of fresh air from the depressing flatness of Soviet reality, a witness to the spirit of "true" Russia and an authentic miracle of spiritual survival. About Solzhenitzyn's attitude to Russia, Fr Alexander coined a great word: the author of the *Gulag Archipelago* and of *August 14* had a "seeing" or "lucid" love of Russia, as opposed to the "blind" nationalism of so many. Fr Schmemann was particularly indignant at those — Russian and western — critics of Solzhenitzyn, who saw in him precisely that "blind" nationalism, which the criticism of pre-revolutionary Russia in *August 14* refutes so obviously. However, Fr Schmemann also responded negatively to some of Solzhenitzyn's enthusiasms, for instance his (passing) admiration for the Old Believers.

Be it as it may, it seems to me that if there is a talent which Fr Alexander did not have the time to develop fully in his published writings, it is his extraordinary grasp of Russian literature (and western, particularly French), his ability to discern what was "true" and what was "false." His few writings (and lectures) on literary topics were among the best in his entire legacy.

A full biography could mention other aspects of Fr Schmemann's career: his involvement, still in France, as Vice-Chairman of the Youth Department of the World Council of Churches, and his brief passage in the "Faith and Order Commission," his lecturing as Adjunct Professor at Union, at General and at Columbia; his later involvement with more conservative Christian circles (the "Hartford Appeal").

A great master of the spoken word, a man able, better than anyone, to relate and to sympathize authentically, but first and foremost a priest committed to the Church always seen, in spite of all human deficiencies, as an anticipation of the Kingdom and as the only authentic token of immortality, Fr Alexander Schmemann occupied so great a place in the life of so many! His legacy will not disappear, not only because his friends will not forget him, but because he obviously remains in the Eternal Memory of God, as a faithful servant in this vineyard.

Index